Presidential Lies

Presidential Lies

The Illustrated History of White House Golf

Shepherd Campbell and Peter Landau

Macmillan•USA

MACMILLAN
A Simon & Schuster Macmillan Company
1633 Broadway
New York, NY 10019

A catalog record is available from the Library of Congress.

ISBN 0-02-861258-2

10 9 8 7 6 5 4 3 2 1

Printed in the United States of America

Book Design by Anne Scatto

Cover Photo Credits
Front: Nixon, Kennedy: UPI/Bettmann;
Eisenhower: AP/Wide World Photos
Back: Reagan: Courtesy, The Ronald Reagan Library;
Taft: Courtesy, The Library of Congress;
Bush and Quayle: AP/Wide World Photos

In Memory of Our Parents

Cornelia S. Campbell   Charlotte Landau

Morgan S. Campbell   Edward Landau

Contents

Presidential Lies

CHAPTER 1

INTRODUCTION

Why Is Golf the Game of Presidents?

T
he moment came, or so the story goes, in England during the spring of 1877. A carriage touring the countryside outside London had chanced upon a golf course, and it paused while the passengers watched a group of golfers fashion a few shots. One of the passengers, an American, turned to his host and inquired, "That looks like good exercise, but what's the little white ball for?"

The puzzled American was Ulysses S. Grant, then beginning a round-the-world trip following his retirement from the U.S. presidency. Grant, thus, is believed to have been the first President in or out of office to witness the game of golf. He was not sufficiently inspired to take up the sport himself, however, which was just as well since golf really didn't take root back home in the United States until 1888, three years after his death. But a remarkable number of his successors in the White House did pursue the game, beginning with the first presidential golf zealot, William Howard Taft, early in the 20th century.

As Presidents came and went during the ensuing decades—through boom times and bad times, through periods of national euphoria, international crises and even war—there seemed to be one

Presidents at Play: Three Chief Executives shared a round together for the first time ever when George Bush, Gerald R. Ford and Bill Clinton met in February 1995 at Indian Wells, California. REUTERS/BETTMANN

near-constant at work in the White House: Golf was more often than not the incumbent's primary form of recreation and relaxation. Some, like Dwight D. Eisenhower, even practiced on the White House grounds. In fact, an involvement with the game is one of the characteristics that has most united the nation's Chief Executives, no matter what their parties, since Taft's time. Golf has been an obsession for some, a diversion for others and a matter of indifference to only a few. Comedian Bob Hope, who golfed with many Presidents, remarked that "my experience with [them] has been that they can take kidding about themselves. Their golf games are something else."

Between the time that Taft entered the White House in 1909 and the Bill Clinton years of the 1990s, there have been 16 Presidents, and no fewer than 13 of them played golf with at least some degree of seriousness. (The three who spurned the links were Herbert Hoover, Harry Truman and Jimmy Carter, as described in chapter 15.) It says something about the bond between golf and the

White House that, when in 1994 a team competition was inaugurated between U.S. and non-European professionals, the new event was called the Presidents Cup.

Presidential Lies examines in detail the surprising role that the game has played in the lives of those 13 golfing Presidents. In the process, it provides a sporting counterpoint to their presidencies—revealing a human, engaging side of these men that rarely emerges from the history texts. It recounts the many amusing, distressing and embarrassing moments they experienced while golfing—something they have in common with all who struggle with the game. This book also tells how the Presidents worked golf into their busy political lives, divulges how well (or poorly) they played and explains how some of them influenced the evolution of the sport in America. And, most important, it describes how they approached the game and what that says about them.

"Sports do not build character," observed author and broadcaster Heywood Hale Broun. "They reveal it." And perhaps no sport reveals its participants' characters more piteously than golf. It puts on display their self-control, the way their minds and muscles work together, how they treat others and how they respond when the pressure is on—all vital qualities to know about a President. Pro star Jimmy Demaret once went so far as to suggest that "if the people wish to determine the best candidate [for President], put all the contenders on a golf course. The one who can take five or six bad holes in a row without blowing his stack is capable of handling the affairs of the nation."

The Lure of the Links

What is it about the royal and ancient game that has made it the sport of choice for most of the Presidents in this century? Is the answer found in the British saying that "golf is the sport of busy men"? Is there something about the office that calls for the qualities found in an avid golfer? Or is there something about the game that attracts those with the intensity of ambition and competitive drive required to make it to the top of the political world?

The lure of the links has been explained in many ways. The leader of another nation, Prime Minister Arthur J. Balfour of Great Britain, once said, "The wit of man has never invented a pastime to equal golf for its healthful recreation, its pleasurable excitement and its never-ending source of amusement." Pulitzer Prize–winning novelist John Updike put it more poetically: "What a beautiful thing a golf swing is, what a bottomless source of instruction and chastisement! . . . Was ever any sporting motion so fraught with difficulty and mystery?"

A more prosaic explanation for the appeal of the game is suggested by a popular wisecrack: "My worst day on the golf course still beats my best day in the office."

Those who've occupied the Oval Office might argue that point. But it begins to get to the core of why the game has attracted so many enthusiasts at the White House. It is principally because golf has seemed to offer, more satisfactorily than anything else, a way for most Presidents to get a complete and refreshing break from the pressures of their office. It acts, in effect, as an 18-hole safety valve.

Club Case: A display at the Burning Tree Club in Bethesda, Maryland, showcases woods used by (from top to bottom) Presidents Taft, Wilson, Harding, Roosevelt, Eisenhower, Kennedy, Johnson, Nixon, Ford and Bush.

COURTESY, THE BURNING TREE CLUB

The authors posed the question of why so many Presidents have loved golf to several former Chief Executives. George Bush replied, "I guess there's no other job like the American presidency. It's hard to leave it, hard to get away from it, hard to relax. Golf helps an awful lot. It's a wonderful way to concentrate on a game and, thus, avoid some of the frustrations of the job."

For his part, Gerald R. Ford responded that golf is popular among Presidents for "the same reason that it attracts people on a broad basis. It's enjoyable, you meet a lot of nice people, golf courses are nice places, and [the game] is competitive. And I think most Presidents are competitive or they wouldn't be there."

But it may be that golf legend Arnold Palmer said it best. "Golf," he declared, "is a way of testing ourselves while enjoying ourselves."

Perhaps the most demanding test in the annals of presidential golf came in February 1995 when Ford, Bush and Clinton met in the pro-amateur event of the Bob Hope Chrysler Classic at Indian Wells, California (see chapter 14). It was the first time that three Presidents had played golf together, and the media interest was intense. With the national press and NBC-TV looking on, each President demonstrated his own golfing style. The gregarious Clinton, jabbering away and working the crowd, golfed at a relaxed pace. Bush, known for his fast play, tried to keep the match moving and sometimes putted out before any of the other players had reached the green. Ford, associated with wandering shots that struck spectators, obliged once more.

"Fore! Fore!" an alarmed Ford hollered on the first tee as his opening drive hooked into the gallery. It didn't hit anyone, but just wait. Sure enough, on the eighth hole, his second shot struck a woman on the hand. Bush, though, did more damage than Ford to spectators. On the first hole, he, too, stroked a ball that veered off course. It ricocheted off a tree and hit 71-year-old Norma Earley on the bridge of her nose. When Bush reached her to apologize, Earley told him, "I'm sorry I got in the way of your shot." But it required 10 stitches to close her cut. Later, Bush hit another spectator, John C. Wrynd, on the back of his thigh. "How's the wound?" Bush asked as he apologized again. "No blood, no problem," Wrynd replied. Bush autographed the errant ball for him.

After watching all this from her home in Houston, Bush's wife, Barbara, commented dryly: "As if we don't have enough violence on television."

The Sport of Kings, Too

It's significant that golf has had much the same appeal for foreign leaders as it has for U.S. Presidents. It all began with King James IV of Scotland in the early 16th century. His successors continued playing the game—including his granddaughter, Mary Queen of Scots, who is widely regarded as the first woman golfer in history. Mary, though, got bad notices in 1567 for playing golf a day or so after one of her husbands was murdered. It was her son, King James VI, who began to push golf beyond the Scottish borders. When he succeeded to the English throne as King James I in 1603, he took his golf clubs with him to London and launched the process that would in time carry the sport around the world.

Through the years, many other British monarchs were keen golfers. But none was keener than King Edward VIII (who before he ascended the throne had been the Prince of Wales and after he abdicated it after only 11 months in 1936 became the Duke of Windsor). He took up the game at age 14, at one point pared his handicap to 11 and competed in numerous U.S. pro-am events. He also cultivated some of golf's great players.

Once, as the Prince of Wales, he invited top U.S. professionals Walter Hagen and Gene Sarazen to lunch with him at the Royal St. George's Golf Club in Sandwich, England. After they were seated, the steward came up and whispered to the prince that the rules of the club barred golf professionals from the dining room. The future king of England glared at the steward and snapped, loud enough to be heard all around the room, "You stop this nonsense or I'll take the Royal out of St. George's." That became a milestone for the game of golf. Hagen and Sarazen not only got treated royally thereafter but, when word of the incident spread,

White House Range: Dwight D. Eisenhower used the South Lawn to work on his iron shots. Ike could hone other parts of his game on the putting green, with a sand trap, right outside the Oval Office. AP/WIDE WORLD PHOTOS

professionals began to get more respectful treatment in clubhouses around the world.

The prince also befriended Crown Prince Hirohito of Japan and introduced the future emperor to golf when he visited Great Britain in 1921. Hirohito was so taken with the game that when he returned to Tokyo he had a nine-hole course built on the grounds of the Imperial Palace. There, he diligently followed the Prince of Wales' example, even wearing a suit of plus-fours with the same tweed patterns that his new British friend sported.

Among the more recent members of British royalty, Princess Anne expressed a distaste for golf, announcing that "I prefer to take the dogs out." But her brother, Prince Andrew, became the family's first real golf addict since the Duke of Windsor. Within three years of taking up the game, Andrew got his handicap down to 15. The time required away from home to accomplish that was, according to press reports, one factor contributing to the separation from his wife, the Duchess of York (a.k.a. "Fergie") in 1992. Andrew, though, could have been speaking for many of those in the public spotlight when he defended golf for "its ability to afford solitude when you only [need] to play a few holes on your own in order to refresh the mind and to escape the madding crowd."

The most zealous royal golfer of recent vintage was King Hassan II of Morocco, who was smitten by the game after 1948 Masters champion Claude Harmon taught him to play. Hassan had a nine-hole course built on his palace grounds. Next to the first tee was a one-room building that had a single chair in the middle of it surrounded by 100 pairs of golf shoes—all the king's. An aide would slip him a pair to match his clothes before play began. And it could begin at any hour, since the king had the whole layout lighted.

Hassan, moreover, hired a clubmaker to move from England to Morocco just to make clubs for him. He required a lot of them. According to Lee Trevino, who received a jeweled dagger for winning the king's pro-am tournament one year, Hassan "had three or four sets of clubs with him and a couple of caddies" during their round. "He had servants walking right down the fairway carrying trays of water, soft drinks and food."

The Best of Them All

Certainly the best golfer ever among kings, princes, prime ministers or presidents was King Leopold III of Belgium. He was so good and so confident of his game that he became the first and only national leader to take part in national golf championships. Not only that, he performed impressively when he did, which was during the years immediately before and after World War II.

In the 1939 Belgian Open Amateur Championship, for example, Leopold made it easily through the stroke-play qualifying stage and then, in the match play stage, went all the way to the 19th hole in his last match before he lost. And 10 years later, he made it to the quarterfinals of the French Open Amateur Championship. But perhaps King Leopold's finest golfing hour came during a 1946 tournament in Switzerland, where he boldly took on leading pros and amateurs on an unfamiliar course. The king finished as the top amateur with an aggregate score of 155 for 36 holes.

Avid golfers among recent foreign leaders have included Prime Minister John Major of Great Britain, President François Mitterrand of France, King Juan Carlos of Spain, Prince Rainier of Monaco, King Baudouin of Belgium, President Ferdinand Marcos of the Philippines, Prime Minister Bob Hawke of Australia, President Carlos Saul Menem of Argentina and King Jigme Singye Wangchuk of Bhutan. In some countries, though, the leaders have had to be secretive about their golf. A French Golf Federation official explained why: "The Left has always looked at golf as a snob sport practiced by the enemy class."

That may be changing. What is arguably the ultimate capitalist sport even began making inroads among the leaders of the Communist world as it disintegrated in the late 1980s. When a Swedish entrepreneur opened a golf course in Moscow in 1989, President Mikhail Gorbachev accepted a membership while his rival and successor, Boris Yeltsin, showed up to hit a few balls. And when the first private course opened in China in 1987, Premier Zhao Ziyang practiced for weeks before hitting the ceremonial first ball at the Beijing Golf Club. Soon, some 20 other courses were under construction in China—including a TPC course near Hong Kong that hosted a tournament for international professionals in 1995.

There's one more reason that golf has been the sport of Presidents and so many other national leaders: It is useful as a tool for building important political relationships and sizing up new acquaintances. Foreign dignitaries, for example, were always welcome to join Dwight D. Eisenhower for a round. "The President feels that a game of golf with a prime minister is worth [many] hours at the conference table," said one of Ike's aides. "He doesn't go into conference matters on the course, but he and his visitor get to know one another better and that makes for a better relationship."

Some foreign leaders, of course, have spurned the game, and a prominent member of that group was Prime Minister David Ben-Gurion of Israel. At a news conference in the 1950s, a U.S. newspaperman asked, "Mr. Prime Minister, is it true that you are building a golf course so you can invite President Eisenhower to Israel?"

Ben-Gurion, looking perplexed, whispered to an aide, "What is golf?"

"It's a game," the aide whispered back.

The prime minister then told the newspaperman, "No, I don't play games."

The First Swings

U.S. Presidents began playing the game less than a decade after the first golf club in the country was founded in 1888 in Yonkers, New York, and named St. Andrew's after the revered original in Scotland. It was William McKinley who became the first sitting President to play golf. But it was only a brief dalliance. McKinley took office in 1897, and one measure of how far the game had come was the number of golfers who populated his Cabinet. "It is asserted on the authority of a member of the Cabinet," *The New York Times* reported at the time, "that all the real business of the regular Cabinet meeting is disposed of in three minutes and that the rest of it—an hour or an hour and a half—is largely devoted to talk [of] golf. . . . When the Cabinet drops in to talk about the game, the President's interest is slightly stimulated and he has sometimes been inclined to try the exercise himself. When he has inquired about the 'lingo' of the game he has been discouraged. 'The game requires study,' he is quoted as saying, 'and I have too many other subjects to study.'"

But Garrett Hobart, his Vice President and an early golf enthusiast, persuaded McKinley to try the game when they were on vacation at Lake Champlain during the summer of 1897. It didn't take. The President quickly lost interest and returned to his favorite holiday pastime: sitting under a tree and reading.

*Divots at Camp David: Gerald R. Ford played on the three-tee, one-green mini-course at
the presidential hideaway. The layout was designed for playing short-iron and wedge
shots. A field served for practice with longer clubs.* COURTESY, THE GERALD R. FORD
LIBRARY

Two summers later at Hot Springs, Virginia, however, McKinley
suggested that he might like to have a second run at golf. When
his advisers learned of the idea, they were aghast. "It would be too
undignified for a President," they have been quoted as protesting.
"It could tear down confidence in the administration." When word
got out, *The Boston Evening Record* conducted a reader poll on
whether the President should play golf and found sentiment split
down the middle. In any case, it's reported that McKinley went
ahead and gave the game a second shot—apparently with much the
same unsuccessful result as his earlier attempt.

The golfing community didn't hold it against him. After
McKinley was assassinated in 1901 early in his second term, the
final match of the U.S. Amateur Championship at the Atlantic City
(New Jersey) Country Club was postponed for a week.

Ordinarily, Vice President Hobart would probably have succeeded McKinley and become the first presidential golfer. But

Hobart had died in 1899, to be replaced as Vice President after the next election by Theodore Roosevelt. So Roosevelt assumed the presidency following McKinley's assassination.

The irrepressible Roosevelt pursued a host of sporting interests; he was an outdoorsman, a big-game hunter, a fencer, a wrestler, a boxer and a tennis player. He even spent two years learning jujitsu. About the only thing he wasn't was a golfer. He had tried the game; in fact, he had been a member of the early and short-lived Oyster Bay Golf Club on New York's Long Island. But on the few occasions when Roosevelt ventured out onto the links, he said he got bored with all the walking and the lack of serious exercise. "Golf is for the birds," he said. "Ta hell with making birdies."

So golf's entree at 1600 Pennsylvania Avenue would have to wait. But it was on its way—and on its way to stay.

HOW THE SECRET SERVICE PROTECTS GOLFING PRESIDENTS

"I 've always enjoyed playing golf with a President," said entertainer Bob Hope, who shared rounds with eight of them from Dwight D. Eisenhower to George Bush and Bill Clinton. "The only problem is that there are so many Secret Service men around there's not much chance to cheat."

All those Secret Service men are around because protecting a U.S. President on a golf course presents the agency with one of its most imposing challenges. A President seems more vulnerable to an assassination attempt on a golf course than in almost any other location. As former U.S. Secret Service chief U. E. Baughman wrote, "A golf course is almost a perfect place for an assassination. If a killer is an expert marksman, the high ground at most courses

Watchful Eyes: As George Bush and his partner drove toward their next shots, two of the members of the President's Secret Service detail scanned the horizon for potential trouble.
AP/WIDE WORLD PHOTOS

gives him an excellent shot at objects below. Also, the trees and shrubs that bound fairways afford perfect concealment.

"Then, on a golf course, one knows the exact route the potential victim will take. And the fact that one's putative target plays a course regularly or even fairly regularly gives plenty of opportunity to work out the details of a plan; I mean, one need not rush into one's assassination attempt." Under the conditions on a course, moreover, escape could be relatively easy.

How does the Secret Service protect a President while he's golfing? It used to be simple in the early days. William Howard Taft, for example, was chaperoned on the links by a single agent who trudged along at a respectful distance in the presidential wake. But the need for greater security intensified in later years, so Baughman and his staff developed a system in 1953 for protecting Eisenhower. It's since been refined with the advent of computers and more sophisticated counter-intelligence operations—although the Secret

Service is keeping the specifics a secret. But it's all built on the same premise, which is to keep a President in a kind of protective cocoon as he plays a course.

Here's how the system worked when Ike was in Washington and wanted to get in a round at the Burning Tree Club in Bethesda, Maryland. An hour in advance, an aide in the White House would phone the club on the direct line that had been set up to the office of club professional Max Elbin. A Secret Service detail would then appear to establish a command post in the clubhouse. If the President was playing with a foreign luminary or head of state, the Secret Service had bomb-sniffing German shepherd dogs check out the whole place, including the kitchen.

Guns on the Course

Out on the course, Ike's party was accompanied by a posse of up to seven agents who were dressed as golfers and carried golf bags that contained not clubs but sets of firearms. The agents were connected by walkie-talkies to the command post, which was prepared to supply reinforcements or medical aid in any emergency.

The President's group was preceded by from one to three agents who had high-powered rifles with telescopic sites stashed in their golf bags. The job of these advance scouts was to head for the highest ground ahead, survey the surroundings and flush out any potential assassins. (They even checked out each ball washer in case the plunger might detonate a bomb.) Two other agents, meanwhile, flanked Eisenhower as he played his round, and they, too, had high-powered rifles in their golf bags. With all that firepower, Baughman said, "we could be certain that [the bullets] would carry to any distance that a sharpshooter might snipe from."

Trailing the presidential party were two more agents, one on foot and one in a golf cart that had a machine gun concealed in it. The machine gun was meant to deal with a group of would-be assassins who might try to rush the presidential party. "In such a case," according to Baughman, "a machine gun is the weapon of choice, for it can handle several assassin types at the same time." Always accompanying the party was the so-called "doomsday briefcase," containing the secret codes for launching U.S. nuclear missiles from land, sea and air—giving the President, as it was once said, the option of ordering his nuclear strike "rare, medium or well-done."

In Eisenhower's day, the Secret Service never encountered any would-be assassins on a golf course—at least none they ever talked about. They did, however, come across "several spooners, a flock of neckers and some petters," Baughman said. "But investigation always showed that these couples were out there in the rough for relatively legitimate reasons."

In the clubhouse at the Newport Country Club in Rhode Island, though, the agents had one scare. Eisenhower had gone inside after a round to sip a soft drink and change his shoes. As he crossed a large, circular ballroom to leave the clubhouse, a door burst open and two women rushed up to him. One threw her arms around the President and kissed him. A bit flustered, Eisenhower said, "Thank you, ma'am."

The Secret Service quickly escorted the women away. And it was the last time that Ike changed his shoes in the Newport clubhouse.

CHAPTER 2

WILLIAM HOWARD TAFT
The Presidential Pioneer

T o look at him—all 355 pounds plus of him during his presidency—he seemed as incapable of playing a passable round of golf as he did of completing an Olympic marathon. Something like sumo wrestling, maybe; a finesse game such as golf, never. According to one joke of the day, "If he put a golf ball where he could hit it, he couldn't see it. And if he put the golf ball where he could see it, he couldn't hit it."

True, few if any locker-room scales in any clubhouse in America were equal to the daunting task of calculating his weight. True, he had his caddies tee balls up for him. And true, his mountainous middle prevented him from taking anything more than a short, choppy swing at the ball.

But believe it: William Howard Taft could both see and hit the ball. Not only that, he could hit it consistently and hit it fairly well. One golfing companion during that heyday of corporate trust-busting said that "the President hits a golf ball much as if it were a corporate malefactor." *The Saturday Evening Post* told its readers that when Taft was golfing he was "as earnest about it as a consul asking to be made a Minister."

A Short Stroke: Taft's girth prevented him from taking more than a choppy, abbreviated swing at the ball. It was not "Scotland's bonnie swing," in the words of one observer. THE BETTMANN ARCHIVE

So it was with Taft's one term in the White House between 1909 and 1913 that golf first assumed its role as the favorite sport of almost all of the U.S. Presidents in the 20th century. It was the relaxation the game provided that most appealed to Taft. "The beauty of golf to me is that you cannot play it if you permit yourself to think of anything else," Taft said. "As every man knows who has played the game, it rejuvenates and stretches the span of life."

Taft, though, was more than the first presidential golf fanatic. He was among the first golf fanatics in the entire country. When he lumbered into the White House at age 51, golf was an infant sport in the United States, a pleasurable new diversion that had been imported from Great Britain barely 20 years before. Yet Taft had already been playing the game seriously for nearly 15 years.

As President, he would escape to the links on every possible occasion—at least twice a week in season in Washington, D.C., no matter what appointments had to be reshuffled, and daily on vacation no matter how forbidding the weather. His weight didn't deter him, of course. And neither did the critics who carped that he should have been spending less time on golf and more on governing. In the end, golf may not have been good for Taft politically, but there's no question that Taft was good for golf. The exposure he gave the game was widely credited with stimulating the nation's first golf boom.

Taft liked to describe himself humbly as only a "bumble-puppy" golfer. But he was certainly no bumbler on the course and, given his gigantic size, he was above all no puppy. An occasional partner of Taft's was Walter J. Travis, the first world-class U.S. golfer. And Travis said that the President was too modest about his game: "I know personally scores and scores of golfers who would almost be tempted to sell their immortal souls could they but put up such a game as he does. The President does play a good game—a very good one considering, if I may be allowed to say so, the handicap of avoirdupois."

How He Began

Taft, who friends called "Will," was a self-taught golfer; he never took a lesson in his life. He'd been introduced to golf by a younger brother, Henry, who had been one of the early pioneers of the game. Henry had joined the St. Andrew's Golf Club, then in Yonkers, New York, just a bit too late to qualify for immortality—in golfing circles, anyway—as a member of the original Apple Tree Gang. They were the legendary group that in 1888 organized St. Andrew's, the first permanent golf club in the United States.

In the summer of 1894, Henry Taft persuaded the future President to play a few rounds on the new nine-hole course near the family's summer home in Murray Bay, Quebec, on the north shore of the St. Lawrence River. Taft was immediately smitten and was back out on the links every available day that summer—even though the Murray Bay layout was later described by Taft's son, Charles, as "a horrible hillside course." Through the years, Taft became such a regular at Murray Bay that, as a tribute to him, the club's governors named one of its holes The President.

In the beginning, Taft could drive the ball no more than 125 yards. But as he worked on his game, the distance grew to a consistent 175 yards and an occasional 200 yards. If his swing never became a thing of beauty, it was eminently serviceable. Like many other players of the day, he gripped his club as he would a baseball bat. "His stroke is not Scotland's bonnie swing," one knowledgeable White House correspondent observed. "It is the short swing of the baseball bat. The President is a good example of the ballplayer who, having taken to golf, plays his golf in a baseball way; just because that way comes easily and feels natural, and because golf can be played that way almost as successfully as in the Scottish way."

Taft had a rather erect stance, kept his head still and swung straight through the ball. "And when he has given the ball its smite and sent it sailing on its way," the reporter noted, "he is done. He makes no after poses. He does not slice. Occasionally there is a slight pull in his play, but that would hardly be called a bad fault." As for his putting, it was quite competent. "He may be expected to hold his own on any green anywhere," the reporter added, "no matter how expert his companions."

How good a golfer was Taft?

His deliberate approach to golf and his abbreviated swing generally produced scores in the 90s. But like golfers before or since, Taft suffered the anguish of inconsistency. He was capable of shooting in the high 80s, but could on occasion soar above 100.

There are those who might scoff that Taft's typical scores could hardly have represented, as Travis said, "a good game." But they actually weren't too shabby considering the golfing conditions in the early part of the 20th century. It must be remembered that Taft and his immediate successors in the White House were at a considerable disadvantage compared with today's players. Clubs had wood shafts, the rubber-core ball had just come into general use, and the courses bore little resemblance to today's immaculately groomed fairways and greens.

Even the best golfers' scores during that era were relatively unimpressive when measured against today's norms. After all, in 1909, the year that Taft entered the White House, Tommy McNamara of Boston shot a round of 69 in the U.S. Open to become the first golfer to break 70 in a major competition in this country.

Taft's own equipment was not only fairly primitive; he also packed just seven or eight clubs in his bag. They generally included a driver, a brassie (comparable to a 2-wood), a midiron (about a 2-iron), a pair of mashies (roughly a 5-iron and a 7-iron), a niblick (9-iron) and a putter. So by the standards of the day, Taft's scores could be called respectable. Not bad for someone who, you might say, hit a fat ball.

Weighty Matters

Actually, Taft's weight wasn't that much of a handicap for him on the links—apart from the restrictions it imposed on his swing. And he never seemed to tire on the course. Major Archibald Butt, Taft's military aide and frequent golfing partner, attested that the President could stride through the most grueling round without any sign of strain. "Golf is a game that leads you to walk without realizing you are walking," Taft said. "When you play a game of 18 holes and walk four or five miles, there is only a pleasant feeling of fatigue when you get through."

His weight was offset to a degree by one important asset: Taft was a reasonably good athlete. Aside from being an excellent horseman, he astonished onlookers with the agility and grace he displayed on the dance floor. "He is nimble as a cat on his feet," Butt said.

There is, to be sure, probably no way that anyone of Taft's prodigious proportions could win the White House today when obesity is widely disdained and when the media mercilessly expose the liabilities of all candidates. But Taft's weight obviously wasn't a serious political handicap at the time. It was, however, the subject of many jokes and wisecracks. The most celebrated of them dated to the years between 1901 and 1904 when Taft served as the first U.S. civil governor of the Philippines. He cabled Secretary of War Elihu Root about a trip made on horseback. "Stood trip well," Taft's cable read. "Rode horseback 25 miles to 5,000-foot elevation."

By return cable, Root inquired, "How is the horse?"

Taft, nonetheless, had qualities that won him many admirers. He was bright and diligent, witty and gracious. And happily for

Addressing the Ball: The caption for this photo in Everybody's Magazine *reported that "often, his fellow golfers say, the President stands and talks to his ball before playing."*
ROBERT LEE DUNN

Taft, his circle of admirers included the most important politician of the day: President Theodore Roosevelt, who hand-picked Taft, then his secretary of war, as the Republican nominee in 1908 to succeed him in the White House.

In Roosevelt's eyes, Taft had only one failing: his well-publicized infatuation with golf. The former Rough Rider's taste in recreation, as noted previously, ran to more vigorous pursuits. He had tried golf and found it too "tame."Along the presidential campaign trail in 1908, though, Taft took regular breaks for rounds of golf and even expounded on the merits of the game to crowds in the Middle West. Mail began descending on Roosevelt's White House criticizing this preoccupation with golf. That was too much for Roosevelt.

"It would seem incredible," he wrote Taft, "that anyone would care one way or the other about your playing golf, but I have received literally hundreds of letters from the West protesting about it. I myself play tennis, but that game is a little more familiar; besides, you never saw a photograph of me playing tennis. I'm careful about that; photographs on horseback, yes; tennis no. And golf is fatal."

Despite Taft's political debt to Roosevelt, he not only ignored his benefactor's advice completely but took public exception to it. In a speech at Wolsey, South Dakota, for instance, Taft told his audience, "They said that I have been playing golf this summer, and that it's a rich man's game, and that it indicated I was out of sympathy with the plain people. I want to state my case before the bar of public opinion on the subject of that game of golf. . . . It is a game for people who are not active enough for baseball or tennis, or who have too much weight to carry around to play those games; and yet when a man weighs 295 pounds [he indulged himself in some harmless campaign hokum with that low a figure] you have to give him some opportunity to make his legs and muscles move, and golf offers that opportunity."

Taft's stubborn allegiance to golf didn't seem to cost him many votes on election day. He won over William Jennings Bryan quite handily by a margin of 321 votes to 162 in the electoral college.

Where He Played

During the four years that Taft was in the White House, he stopped visiting Murray Bay in Canada for summer holidays, bowing to the precedent that then prohibited a sitting President from leaving U.S. soil. But that, of course, in no way inhibited his golf. When in Washington, he played at the Chevy Chase Club nearby in Maryland, where the club history recalls he was "a man who could and did put aside the artificial barriers of his high office. . . . His affectionate nature and jovial personality endeared him to all."

For years, Chevy Chase members retold the story of Taft's reaction when he first saw the new clubhouse that was under construction in 1911. The exterior stone work had just been completed, and the new building stood stark and bare, unadorned by any landscaping. The President's immediate verdict: "It's the finest example of early penitentiary architecture I have ever seen." The members forgave him for that and even for the time he allowed his son, Charles, to play a round with him there while wearing baseball spikes.

Away from Washington, Taft played at home at the Cincinnati Country Club, where he had been elected as the first club president in 1902. But more frequently during his presidential years, he vacationed in Beverly, Massachusetts, where the family had taken a summer home and where he could golf on the Myopia Hunt Club course, which was considered one of the finest in the country. It was also considered one of the most demanding. It was usually swept by stiff sea breezes off the Atlantic Ocean, and there were 109 traps and bunkers lying in wait. Its greens, moreover, were especially perverse. One member likened putting on them to "playing billiards with the cloth off."

Taft liked to tell of the time he encountered two friends who had just completed a round at Myopia and inquired how they'd done. They told him, "the first hole was won in 18 to 19, the second in

23 to 26, the third in 11 to 13"—and then things had gone down-hill from there. When Taft asked who'd won, one of the shell-shocked duffers claimed that he had because he'd lost only six balls as against his opponent's seven.

During the President's first summer at Myopia, some of the members fell to speculating about whether he could break 100 on the formidable course. Some wagers were proposed, and before long $1,000 was riding on Taft's next round. He proved equal to the challenge and posted a heroic 98. "It was a rattling good score for the middle-class player," Butt wrote in a letter. "I have never seen him so happy over anything. . . . Mrs. Taft takes the greatest inter-est in his game always, and the news that he had made it under 100 made her most happy. She went up to him and kissed him when she heard it—a mark of great favor from Mrs. Taft, for she is not demonstrative as a rule in public."

Why He Fled to the Links

As President, Taft played golf for more than exercise. It also became a pleasurable form of escapism. He discovered he did not enjoy the unrelenting demands of the office. So while he worked hard, the President would flee to the golf course at every opportunity. And he didn't like any interruptions, as anyone who approached him there on a political or governmental matter quickly learned.

When an official at the State Department asked Taft to meet the president of Chile, who was visiting Washington, the President snapped, "I'll be damned if I will give up my game of golf to see this fellow." And when Taft was frustrated in his dealings with Congress on the landmark Payne-Aldrich tariff bill, his reaction was typical. "They have my last word," he fumed, "and now I want to show my scorn for further negotiations by spending the afternoon on the golf links." The ploy, however, didn't work; Taft failed to get the bill he wanted.

Even some golfers managed to offend him. "We are considerably troubled by persons wanting to get" a game with the President, Butt wrote in a letter. "Colonel Fred Crosby was the latest

Setting Priorities: Golf ranked so high among Taft's interests that he once said, "I'll be damned if I will give up my game of golf" to meet the visiting president of Chile. COURTESY, THE LIBRARY OF CONGRESS

applicant. The President granted his request to take him on for a game but was so displeased with the letter asking for the engagement that he is not likely to accord him another game. He began his letter 'Dear Taft,' and the intimacy, in view of the President's position, did not warrant such familiarity." Butt continued, "I think it will be the last opportunity the handsome colonel will get to be advertised as a golf companion of the President." (Tragically, Butt would go down with the *Titanic* late in Taft's term.)

What was it like to play a round with Taft?

By all accounts, he was the most amiable of golfing colleagues— at least when he wasn't being pestered. Sir Harry Lauder, the roving Scottish minstrel who once played with the President, said he found him "the finest tonic against the blues in all America. We had a great game of golf together at Augusta, Georgia, and I took the liberty of beating the President by two holes. . . . But he smiled all the time; in fact, I don't think I have ever met a man with so dominating a smile. He simply exuded geniality."

Another partner, champion golfer Travis, offered further insights into Taft's game when he recalled a match that he, the President and two presidential aides played at the Chevy Chase Club in June 1910. As always, the President was accompanied by a single Secret Service agent and was granted a perquisite he insisted upon: a two-hole distance between his party and any following golfers.

On the first hole at Chevy Chase, Travis said, "the President got his par 3 by hitting a very good tee shot followed by a fine approach and a superb downhill putt of eight yards." At the second tee, Taft said, "I don't think I can keep up this pace." And he couldn't. He topped his drive. But he came back on the 344-yard third hole with a solid par 4. So it went on succeeding holes with Taft seeming to tolerate the good with the bad—the delights of pars offset by the frustrations of double bogeys—until the last hole.

"It was on this hole that the President betrayed the one and only outward sign of irritation during the entire match," Travis said. "Unlike most of us, he is imperturbable over his mistakes, philosophically accepting them as part of the game. On the other hand, he is visibly pleased when he makes a particularly good shot, frequently indulging in a hearty, whole-souled laugh."

On the 18th at Chevy Chase, Taft lined up an easy putt and missed it. Worse, he then failed to sink the tap-in. "Scores, hundreds, nay thousands of men have been known, under like circumstances, to say and do things that cannot be repeated," Travis noted. But all Taft did was to mutter with an air of mild disgust, "Oh, pshaw!"

But Taft's composure on the course masked an intense determination. "Every stroke is played as though he were a James Braid or a Harry Vardon competing for the world's championship," Travis wrote, referring to two British stars of the day. The President "never gives up. No matter how darkly the goddess of golf may frown upon his efforts, he still strives his hardest to regain her favor, playing the game for all he is worth all the time. And when he has holed out, whether it be a 3 or a 7, the score is duly recorded in his scorebook without any exultation on the one hand or hard luck stories on the other." (The President always kept score in a little red notebook so that he could compare his results with previous rounds and track his progress.)

Taft was invariably game for more. After the Travis match, the President asked, "Brother Travis, what are you going to do tomorrow?" Travis replied that, unfortunately, he had already arranged to return to New York that night.

That wouldn't wash with the President. So another match was scheduled for the following morning. The entire 18 holes were played in a downpour, which Taft simply shrugged off ("It's got to rain great guns," said one observer, "to keep him from his golf"). The President just donned the heavy sweater he kept for such occasions and proceeded to slog around the course in three fewer strokes than he had the previous day.

An Illegal Putter?

The clubs that Taft carried were fairly long and heavy, especially the irons. His wood-shafted driver and brassie each measured about 47 inches and weighed some 14 ounces. For putting, he used the center-shafted Schenectady model, a controversial club that was popular in the United States. But it had been outlawed by the Royal and Ancient Golf Club of St. Andrews, Scotland, after Travis had made it famous by using one when he won the British Amateur championship in 1904. The R&A rulemakers contended that the putter's mallet-head shape provided a player with an unsporting advantage and for nearly 50 years forbade its use in championships held on British soil.

Travis himself pointed out the ban in a long letter to Taft, but the President refused to budge. On December 11, 1911, he dictated this reply from the White House:

My Dear Mr. Travis:

I have yours of Dec. 7. I think the restriction imposed by St. Andrews is too narrow. I think putting with a Schenectady putter is sportsmanlike, and gives no undue advantage.

Sincerely yours,
William H. Taft

The issue created such a stir in the burgeoning world of U.S. golf that *The New York Times* was moved to take an editorial position on it. The paper noted that "President Taft, who is a fairly competent golfer," had come out "in favor of the mallet-like Schenectady putter in defiance of the edict of Scottish golfers." And backing the U.S. position, the *Times* concluded, "The skill is not in the club. The art of putting is harder to master than Greek or calculus. But once mastered, the old-fashioned gun metal club, the gooseneck and the Schenectady serve equally well."

Taft's frequent golfing forays from the White House attracted the attention of the national press right from the beginning of his term. For the next four years, newspapers and magazines carried frequent articles about his golf, illustrated with photographs of him playing. Political cartoonists delighted in showing him in golf settings. That didn't bother the President in the least. One of his favorite cartoons depicted Taft the golfer at the top of his backswing about to strike a ball labeled "Tariff."

But all the publicity proved to be a mixed blessing. On one hand, the free ink was a great boon to the fledgling game of golf. "Many men who otherwise might not have been led to take up the game have done so since Mr. Taft became Chief Executive," Travis wrote in *The Century* midway through Taft's term. "What is good enough for the President is good enough for them." Indeed, one enterprising club manufacturer went so far as to cash in on the President's association with the game by introducing a "Taft putter."

On the other hand, there was a negative flip side to the President's obsession with golf. The attention it received made it appear to some that Taft was lavishing an unseemly amount of time on the game. As a result, the President began to take a lot of heat about his golf. Biographer Judith Icke Anderson wrote about how Washington reporters complained that, apart from the Philippines where he'd been the civil governor, golf seemed to be the only subject the President liked to discuss. They began writing articles that chided him for playing golf when he should have been at work in the Oval Office.

In Taft's home state, *The Ohio State Journal,* for example, commented sardonically that he "hardly gets fairly settled down to golf" before presidential duties interrupt him. *Hampton's* magazine reproached him for letting others champion Republican legislation in Congress while the President's "celebrated smile and a large bag of golf sticks were conveyed each afternoon to the Chevy Chase Golf Links." Finley Peter Dunne had Mr. Dooley, his fictional, wily observer of the American scene, quote Taft as saying, "Golf is th' thing I like best next t' leavin' Washington."

Criticism Hurts

Taft's days as the pioneering White House golfer ended after the 1912 election when he stood for a second term against not only the Democrats' Woodrow Wilson but also Roosevelt, his erstwhile patron. Roosevelt had become disenchanted with Taft's conservative policies (he now derided the President as a man "who means well feebly"), and he formed his own Progressive ("Bull Moose") Party to challenge Taft. It was a frustrating struggle on two fronts for the President. And his frustration showed when he lashed out at his advisers for complaining that his opponents were reaping tons of publicity while "there is no news of me except that I played golf. I seem to have heard that before. It always makes me impatient."

Taft was trounced at the polls but—as a former lawyer, prosecutor and judge—he moved on contentedly to become a law professor at his alma mater, Yale. His golf clubs, needless to say, were seldom out of reach, and his wife, Nellie, now joined him on the course

From a drawing by E.W. Kemble in "Harper's Weekly," March 6, 1909.
"Good-by, Bill, I've had a perfectly corking time."

A Sporting Transition: In this contemporary editorial cartoon, Theodore Roosevelt (left) is shown retiring from the White House with assorted athletic gear while Taft enters with his golf clubs.

occasionally. Then, in 1921, the one job he'd always coveted opened up: Chief Justice of the U.S. Supreme Court. It seemed almost certain that President Warren G. Harding would offer him the appointment but, as Taft put it, "I'll wait until the golf ball is in the hole." A few days later it was.

In those post-presidential years, Taft peeled off some of his surplus poundage. As Chief Justice, he slimmed down to 244 pounds—his weight in college—thanks to serious dieting and lots of stalking around golf courses. He continued to play until the age of 70 when his physician ruled out golf because of a heart condition. So Taft passed his last summer at Murray Bay in 1929 sitting on the clubhouse porch and watching golfers tee off.

It was a melancholy way to hole out. But among his legacies, William Howard Taft left something special: a tradition of golf in the White House, one that would endure for the rest of the century—and undoubtedly beyond.

THE PRESIDENT-ELECT
AND THE BILLIONAIRE

They made an unlikely pairing—the portly, amiable President-elect and the gaunt, laconic, richest man in the world. But they had one thing in common, besides an affinity for power: Golf was their mutual obsession.

William Howard Taft and John D. Rockefeller came, briefly, to be golf buddies of a sort late in 1908 at the Bon Air Hotel in

Shared Obsession: Taft traded golf talk with oil tycoon John D. Rockefeller (right) while the two were vacationing in Georgia.

AP/WIDE WORLD PHOTOS

Augusta, Georgia, where Taft had sought seclusion to ponder his Cabinet choices and to relax on the course after winning that year's presidential election.

Rockefeller had taken up the game late in life for therapeutic reasons and attacked it with such fervor that he had private courses installed at two of his estates. He applied himself diligently to the game and was generally able to score in the 90s. (He cured a tendency to raise his left foot on his backswing by having his caddie press a croquet wicket down over it before each shot.)

Every morning at the hotel, *Collier's* magazine reported, "the richest man in the world goes knocking a little white ball (cost, 50 cents) with a stick (cost, $3) over the fields and every afternoon he does the same thing. . . . Out of golf hours, he mixes with the hotel guests and he tells stories."

During one such session, Taft entered the room and the other guests gradually drifted over to hear him talk about that day's golf round.

"I was sorry I could not get near enough to hear you," Rockefeller told Taft later.

"I did an 88 today," the President-to-be announced triumphantly.

The two then fell into conversation, according to *Collier's,* about "the one subject they had in common—the chase of the little white ball. They had frequently been on the golf course at the same time" but had never played together. Rockefeller, "when he made a good drive, celebrated with that brown, withered-apples smile which has left so many financiers in doubt. And the big man with his rapid stride, when he made a good stroke, broke into that ringing laugh which has left so many gentlemen in doubt as to who are to be in the Cabinet. . . . The atmosphere was golfo-political."

CHAPTER 3

WOODROW WILSON
The Crisis Golfer

A s legend has it, Woodrow Wilson was engrossed in a round of golf at Princeton, New Jersey, on a late summer afternoon in 1910 when a messenger came scurrying up the fairway. Everyone in the golf party knew that he was bringing word on whether or not Wilson had won the Democratic nomination for governor of New Jersey at the party's convention then meeting in Trenton. But Wilson waved the messenger off and insisted on finishing the hole. Only after he sank his putt did he turn to hear the news that he had, in fact, secured the nomination.

That was the kind of golfing intensity Wilson brought with him to the White House a few years later. During most of his two terms (1913 to 1921), he could be found eagerly pursuing the game at critical moments in his presidency. Wilson was on the links, for instance,

- When he learned in 1914 that the Mexican government had refused to apologize for its arrest of U.S. sailors at Tampico. He broke off play at a Virginia course to write an ultimatum that threatened military action against the Mexicans. War was averted, however, when tempers cooled.

Devoted Duffer: Wilson didn't play well, but he did play often—more, when he was healthy, than any other President.

THE NATIONAL ARCHIVES

- When he received the stunning news in 1915 that a German submarine had sunk the *Lusitania,* a Cunard liner, with the loss of 128 American lives. Wilson left a course in Maryland immediately and convened a crisis meeting with his Cabinet at the White House.

- Two days after the presidential election of 1916 when the outcome of his close race for a second term against Charles Evans Hughes was still undecided. As he played the back nine, a bystander inquired, "How's your game, Mr. President?" Wilson replied, "I'm three down, but I don't care. I'm four states up in the election."

- On the morning in 1917 before he appeared at a joint session of Congress to ask for authority to declare war on Germany and, thus, to enter the United States into World War I. He was on the course the next day, too.

- Just before he subsequently addressed Congress proposing war against Germany's ally, the Austro-Hungarian Empire.
- On the morning of the day in 1918 that he resolved a sticky predicament by pardoning a particularly militant band of suffragettes. They had provoked a national outcry—and had been jailed—after picketing the White House with signs that accused Wilson of failing to champion voting rights for women.

If all that makes it appear Wilson was forever out golfing, it's not far from wrong. He unquestionably spent more of his presidential hours on golf courses, before he suffered a stroke in 1919, than any Chief Executive before or since. In fact, Wilson golfed year-round and liked to boast that he played six times a week during the summer.

How did he manage that? By rising early on most weekday mornings (sometimes at 5 or 6 A.M.) and squeezing in nine or more holes at a nearby course. Often, he would carry his own Sunday bag containing a hickory-shafted driver, a driving cleek, a midiron, a lofter and a thin-bladed putter. Wilson would still be at his desk in the Oval Office by midmorning. On Saturdays, he typically played a full round of 18 holes, often in the afternoon. And the weather conditions, except on the rawest winter days, were irrelevant. If it was raining, he didn't mind. If it was cold, he wore his cap and his favorite sweater with a moth hole in it. If there was snow on the ground, he played with golf balls painted red by his Secret Service detail and left to dry beside a White House furnace.

Missing Fundamentals

Did all that play produce impressive scores? Alas, it did not. Wilson was a hacker in the true sense of the word. One journalist reported that the President "was a fidgety player who addressed the ball as if he would reason with it." He used a baseball grip and, the journalist continued, "never learned the fundamental necessity of following through. Quite often he sliced in a way that would bring tears to the eyes of his caddie." Even though his short game and

putting were fairly respectable, Wilson rarely if ever broke 100 and generally shot about 115. He once took a 26 at the second hole of the Washington Golf & Country Club across the Potomac River in Arlington, Virginia, because he was unable to make his ball stick on the small, domed green.

No wonder he once defined golf, in the most quoted presidential comment on the game, as "an ineffectual attempt to put an elusive ball into an obscure hole with implements ill-adapted to the purpose." (A somewhat similar quotation has been attributed to Winston Churchill.)

There were a number of reasons for Wilson's deficiencies on the links. He had never been much of an athlete, he didn't begin to play the game until he was in his 40s, he never approached golf competitively, and he had poor vision out of his right eye as a result of a retinal hemorrhage. That meant he had a restricted view of the ball when he swung. "My right eye is like a horse's," he explained. "I can see straight out with it, but not sideways. As a result, I cannot take a full swing because my nose gets in the way and cuts off my view of the ball."

But scratch golf wasn't Wilson's goal; amusement and exercise were. He did take instruction at one stage from Charles Lewis, an itinerant English pro whose eminent pupils at various times also included British Prime Minister Arthur J. Balfour, the Duke of Windsor and King George VI. Lewis's lessons didn't really help, but that failed to dampen the President's enthusiasm. Colonel Edward T. Brown, an old friend from Georgia and an occasional golfing partner, said that Wilson was "cheerful and wholesome under any and all circumstances and a delightful companion always. . . . When he has made a particularly fine drive or accomplished a difficult approach or is complimenting an opponent on a clever putt, you wouldn't think he had a care in the world."

Wilson first played as a professor at Princeton in 1898 and continued to golf occasionally when he went on to become the president of Princeton and governor of New Jersey. He used a set of clubs that Cleveland Dodge, a close friend and wealthy Princeton trustee, had brought back for him from Scotland—but not without some difficulty in getting them past the authorities. At customs, a suspicious inspector listened skeptically as Dodge tried to explain what the clubs were. Finally, Dodge attempted a demonstration. But the inspector interrupted him, saying, "I'll just put them down as agricultural implements."

Doctor's Orders

Wilson didn't play with any real frequency, however, until he occupied the White House—and then it was under doctor's orders. By the time he assumed the presidency, the lean, scholarly Wilson had suffered digestive and stress problems for years. He actually brought to the White House a stomach pump and coal-tar headache tablets, both of which he had used periodically. His fragile health hardly seemed up to the demands of his new office. So Dr. Cary Grayson, the White House physician Wilson inherited from Taft, immediately put him on a healthier diet and insisted on a program of daily exercise that consisted principally of golf.

To make sure that Wilson put in the prescribed amount of time on local links, the doctor signed himself up as the President's permanent partner. It was a good pairing. Joseph E. Murphy, the chief of the White House detail of the Secret Service, was once asked how well Wilson played. Murphy's response was brutally succinct: "He's terrible. So is Grayson."

Nonetheless, the golf and the new diet soon restored Wilson's vigor. In the process, he came to appreciate the game even more. In fact, he wrote one friend from the White House in 1914 that "my chief real interest is golf. It seems to put oxigen [*sic*] into my heart." And he explained in a letter to another friend that "while you are playing, you cannot worry and be preoccupied with affairs. Each stroke requires your whole attention and seems the most important thing in life. I can by that means get perfect diversion of my thoughts for an hour or so at the same time that I am breathing the pure out-of-doors."

While Wilson and Grayson each had flawed games, they had fun together. The President, a talented mimic, developed an amusing routine that he called "Grayson Approaching a Golf Ball." They also shared an adventure or two. During a holiday in the South, for example, they were walking back from a round of golf when they spotted something alarming atop a house they were passing. After they laid down their clubs and knocked at the door, the lady who opened it gushed, "Oh, Mr. President, it's so good of you to call on me. Won't you come into the parlor and sit down?"

"I haven't got the time," Wilson replied. "Your house is on fire!" He and Grayson then rushed up to the attic where they put out the small blaze before the local firemen arrived.

Other than Grayson and sometimes Colonel Brown and Stockton Axson (the brother of Wilson's first wife, Ellen), the President had few golfing partners—until he was joined in 1915, more than a year after his first wife's death, by his new spouse, Edith Bolling Wilson. She became the first and, until late in the century at least, the only First Lady who could truly be considered a golfer. (See the end of this chapter.)

Wilson received some criticism for golfing in relative seclusion—for failing to invite senators, representatives and other members of Washington officialdom to play with him. Other presidential golfers have indulged such partners. Why didn't Wilson? "The fact of the matter is that he did not want business mingled with his recreation," Grayson explained in his memoirs, "and he soon found that most men whom he invited to play with him insisted on introducing public business into the conversation. He did one thing at a time. When he worked, he worked to the exclusion of everything from his mind except the matter in hand, and he carried the same spirit into his diversions."

The presidential mood, weighed down by the responsibilities of the office, could sometimes be a bit grumpy when Wilson started a round—as it was one day when Edmund W. Starling of the Secret Service acted as his caddie because none of the regular caddies were available. On one early hole, Wilson drove the ball only about 50 yards from the tee. As he addressed his second shot, a boy standing on the edge of the fairway cupped his hands to his mouth and made a series of Indian calls. Wilson stepped back from the ball, leaned

Deft Touch: His approach shots and putting were fairly respectable and the strongest parts of Wilson's game.
COURTESY,
THE WOODROW
WILSON HOUSE

on his club and said in a disgusted manner, "That boy must be training to be a senator. He is always making a noise with his mouth and not saying anything!"

The President then topped the ball, which this time traveled about 25 yards. His next shot, however, flew far and straight down the fairway. "This tickled him," Starling said, "and his good humor was restored."

It usually took Wilson four or five holes to unwind and forget his official cares. At that point, he could begin telling jokes, often in dialect, that he illustrated with flourishes of a club. Or he would do one of his imitations. Starling recalled the occasion when Edith Wilson "laid her niblick across her husband's shoulders and bent him forward so that it would not slip off. Immediately he changed his stride to imitate the lumbering gait of an ape. When he tired of the jest, he bent forward, let the niblick roll over the top of his head and caught it as it fell."

Wilson, thus, was not the austere academic that he often appeared. He had a facile and sometimes devastating wit. There was the time, when he was governor of New Jersey, that he received a late-night call from the president of the state bar association telling him that the Chief Justice of New Jersey had just died. After a few appropriate words of mourning for the departed Chief Justice, the bar association president said, "Governor, while it may seem unseemly at this time, I should like to suggest myself in his place."

"If it's all right with the undertaker," Wilson answered, "it's certainly all right with me."

Club Controversy

As a rule, Wilson golfed on such courses as those at the Washington Golf & Country Club in Virginia, the Town & Country facility or the old Kirkside Club in Maryland. He spurned the more fashionable Chevy Chase Club in Maryland although he had been offered an honorary membership there, as have all Presidents since Theodore Roosevelt.

That membership, as it happened, was the source of one of the first controversies of the Wilson administration. Initially, the new President turned down the free honorary membership at the Chevy Chase Club. Officially, the reason he gave was that he was too busy to make use of the club. But some of his biographers have suggested the real reason was that, because he was a Democrat, he was reluctant to join a club so associated with the rich and powerful. Club officials, in any case, were stunned by his turndown. And when his first excuse didn't fly, Wilson then said it wouldn't be fair to all the other dues-paying members if he got in gratis.

In the ensuing furor, *The New York Times* editorialized that "it was a mistake [for Wilson] to decline this accustomed courtesy with seeming brusqueness . . . for it involved unnecessarily hurting the feelings of men whose only purpose was to be kind and to show honor where honor was due. . . . His words lent themselves all too readily to interpretation as a proclamation of superior virtue. . . . Honorary membership in a club involves no more in the way of attendance than the recipient finds it convenient to give, so it could not have compelled any neglect of public business, and as to not paying dues, the President need not have worried since not he, but his office, would be exempt."

Finally, after the president of the Chevy Chase Club visited him at the White House, Wilson backed down and accepted the membership. But he seldom, if ever, used it.

The President also avoided another club, the Woodmont Country Club in Rockville, Maryland, but for a more personal reason. When he was playing there in the spring of 1914, he hit a drive on a par-3 hole where the green was not visible from the tee. The group ahead was still on the green, and Wilson's ball narrowly missed hitting one of them. Fulton Brylawski, a club member who was in the group, came storming back, yelling and swearing at whoever the offending golfer had been. He realized too late, to his embarrassment, that it was the President of the United States. Brylawski wrote Wilson an apology, which was accepted. "But," the club history notes wistfully, "Wilson never came back."

And Brylawski, who went on to become the club's handicap champion, was still hearing about the incident years later. When he boarded a local street car, for instance, friends would often teasingly shout "Fore!"

Wilson was never castigated in the press and elsewhere, as Taft had been, for the time he spent playing golf. It may have had something to do with the public perceptions of the two men. Taft was seen as something of a roly-poly gladhander while Wilson's image was that of a scholar/statesman, someone who would never put a diversion ahead of his duties.

War-time Play

There were a few occasions, however, when Wilson backed off from golf. As the pressure built on the United States to enter World War I, for example, the two Wilsons met one morning with the President's closest adviser at that time, Colonel Edward M. House. Wilson was nervously rearranging his library books as the three chatted aimlessly. To break the tension they all felt, Edith Wilson suggested they "might play golf," asking, "Do you think that would make a bad impression, Colonel?"

"I don't think the American people would feel that the President should do anything trivial at a time like this," House replied. So the three went down to the White House basement to play pool.

That was the exception, though. War or no war, Wilson carried on resolutely with his golf. It brought to mind a bit of World War I English doggerel about an imaginary German invasion.

I was playing golf
The day the Germans landed.
All our men had run away and
All our ships were stranded.
And the thought of England's shame
Almost put me off my game.

The Studious Approach: Wilson "was a fidgety player," wrote one journal-ist, "who addressed the ball as if he would reason with it."

THE BETTMANN ARCHIVE

But after the United States entered the conflict in April 1917, some changes had to be made in the President's golf routine in the interest of his security. When he, his wife and Grayson were driven to a course, they were accompanied by two motorcycle policemen and a large car containing a half dozen Secret Service men. On the course, the party was shadowed by the Secret Service detail, which stood behind trees and bushes at a discreet distance.

As the President was teeing off during one round, Edith Wilson recalled, one of the "two little boys who had been following along asked the other, 'Who is them men who don't play?' With much scorn, the other answered, 'Why them's his keepers.' Mr. Wilson said he did not mind muffing his shot."

Other children lined the road to cheer the President and his wife on those mornings when they drove to the Washington Golf & Country Club. As a gesture of thanks, the Wilsons distributed presents to those children during the 1917 Christmas season. "It's difficult to say who had more fun," *The Washington Post* reported, "the kids or the Presidential couple."

Wilson, who would not play through golfers on the course, also refused to accept other favors of any kind. For instance, he was offered a special courtesy during World War I by Dr. Harry Garfield, the head of the government's Commission on Fuel (and the son of former President James Garfield). Dr. Garfield telephoned the White House to say that, while he was banning the use of fuel at country clubs during the approaching winter of 1917 to 1918, he "wished the President to know that [the Commission] would take pleasure in seeing to it that the necessary exemptions are granted to the country clubs at which the President may play golf."

Wilson immediately rejected the idea, instructing his private secretary, Joseph P. Tumulty, to "please say to Dr. Garfield that I would not for anything have him make any exception with regard to the country clubs at which I play golf during the winter. I would not consent in any case, but as a matter of fact, I never make use of the clubhouses." Indeed, the only times he set foot in clubhouses were when he passed through them before or after a round.

Like most of the big-name golfers of the day, moreover, the President pitched in to help raise money for the Red Cross and other war charities. The stars of the game, from Walter Hagen to a young Bobby Jones, played exhibitions for these causes. In addition, the golf balls they used were sometimes auctioned off after a round, a hole or a great putt. Wilson, too, did his part. He autographed golf balls that went at charity auctions for $500 to $650 apiece.

But the President paid painfully for one wartime gesture. A celebrated, battle-scarred British tank, the *Britannia,* was displayed at the White House in the spring of 1918, and Wilson was urged to take a ride in it. He did—to the front gate. As he climbed out of the tank, he grabbed a red-hot pipe that severely burned his right hand. It was bandaged and useless for several weeks. But did that keep him from the golf course? Hardly. He played with just his left arm, prompting his wife to write that "Woodrow is becoming the greatest one-arm champion in the world."

Postwar Decline

Once the war was over, Wilson put an intolerable strain on himself as he struggled to hammer out a peace settlement in Europe and campaigned in vain at home to sell Congress and the U.S. public on joining his proposed international organization, the League of Nations (some Americans thought it was a new baseball league). In fact, for once a crisis kept the President from the golf course. During the critical postwar negotiations in Paris, according to Wilson biographer Gene Smith, "Other great men could go golfing on weekends, but when they returned, always they saw lights burning in [Wilson's] chambers."

Before long, in 1919, the President's health broke. A thrombosis and then a severe stroke left him incapacitated and unable to govern. He lay stricken in his bedroom while, unbeknownst to the nation, the White House was run for the 17 remaining months of his term by Edith Wilson, Grayson and Tumulty.

Some blamed the President's collapse in part on a sudden lack of exercise during the punishing months that followed the war. If nothing else, though, Wilson's last tragic years in the White House verified his own observation that a President "needs to have the constitution of an athlete, the patience of a mother and the endurance of an early Christian."

THE FIRST GOLFING FIRST LADY

It was hardly a romantic encounter. They first met as Woodrow Wilson and his physician, Dr. Cary Grayson, returned to the White House after a round of golf in March 1915. Edith Bolling Galt, as she was then, had been invited over for tea by the President's cousin, Helen Bones, and as the ladies stepped off the elevator, Wilson and Grayson emerged around a corner looking rather grungy in muddy boots and well-worn golf attire. After the introductions, the men tidied themselves up and joined the ladies for tea in the Oval Room. The President and Edith Galt, both of whom had been widowed, discovered that they had much in common—including golf. And a week before Christmas that year, they were married.

They golfed together almost from the beginning and played every morning during their honeymoon at The Homestead, a resort in Hot Springs, Virginia, where their suite overlooked the golf course.

Back at the White House, Edith Wilson immediately joined the President and Grayson on their early morning rounds of golf, making her the first presidential wife to play the game while in the White House.

One morning, she wasn't playing at all well and her elderly caddie, as she told it in her memoirs, "became more and more bored. Finally, I thought to placate the old fellow by asking his advice. When I had a very near approach to the green, I said in my

Playing Partner: On mornings when golf was scheduled (and it was most mornings), Edith Bolling Wilson rose at 6:00 A.M. to have breakfast with her husband and then join him on the links.
COURTESY, THE WOODROW WILSON HOUSE

most beguiling way: 'Do you think I can reach the green with the midiron?'

"'Yes, if you hit it often enough,' he replied."

A handsome, vivacious woman from a distinguished Virginia family, Edith Wilson requested one change in the White House routine that complicated life for the staff. She decided that she and the President would have breakfast upstairs in her room every morning at 6 A.M. before they golfed. "I suggested that the servants leave things ready," she said, "and that I would cook the eggs so they would not have to get up so early. But they insisted on serving us."

Accounts vary widely on Edith Wilson's proficiency as a golfer; she has been described as everything from "inexpert" to "excellent."

She was certainly both of those during one round at Hot Springs. On one par-4 hole, she topped the ball on her second shot and drove it into a patch of mud. Then flailing away, her neat plaid skirt swirling and flying in all directions, she took 17 strokes to dig the ball out.

On another par-4, her drive landed right in front of a rail fence that crossed the fairway. It seemed an impossible lie.

"What club would you like, ma'am?" her caddie asked.

"The putter," she said decisively. That request drew an astonished look from the caddie.

She ignored it and took a powerful swipe at the ball. What happened next sounds improbable. But according to her biographers, the ball shot under the fence, scooted along the fairway, rolled across the green and dropped into the cup—for an eagle!

CHAPTER 4

WARREN G. HARDING
A Lust for the Links

L ike any golfer, Warren G. Harding was always looking for an edge, some small way to help him tame a course. But Harding went farther than most in at least one respect: He liked to take a few nips for the yips.

Every once in a while, he'd pause for a quick shot of whiskey as he made his way around the links at the Chevy Chase Club outside Washington. Club members were scandalized—and with good reason. This was during the early days of Prohibition, and here was the President of the United States, who had only recently sworn to "preserve, protect and defend the Constitution," openly flouting its new 18th Amendment.

The outcry was sufficient to make Harding give up his on-course imbibing at Chevy Chase—but not everywhere. To his rescue came the wealthy and hard-drinking owner of *The Washington Post,* Edward B. McLean, who had a private golf course at his local estate, known as Friendship. McLean invited the President to use the course whenever he wished. There, not only could Harding test his skills against a rugged layout, but a butler would appear about every four holes bearing a tray that contained glasses of iced Scotch-and-sodas for the President and his playing companions.

Crowd Pleaser: Harding, ever the politician, didn't mind when spectators or reporters watched him play. In fact, he performed so well before the press in 1920 that he earned an inflated reputation as a golfer. OHIO HISTORICAL SOCIETY

The handsome, silver-haired Harding was a lot of things: a drinker (but not a drunkard), a charmer, a politician, a gambler, a dandy, a ladies' man and always a loyal friend. But during his two and one-half years in the White House from 1921 to 1923, he was above all a golfer, at least during his off-hours. And he did more than just play. He established the Warren G. Harding Cup as the trophy for the winners of the U.S. Public Links Championship. The U.S. Golf Association thought enough of his commitment to the game to make him an honorary member of its executive committee.

One presidential letter reveals a lot about where Harding's priorities lay. Jay E. House of *The Philadelphia Ledger* had offered him some golf tips, and in gratitude Harding wrote, "A great many people tell me what to do, but so few of them tell me precisely how to do it. You have told me how to reduce my golf scores. Now that is real and very valuable advice!"

The President, plainly, was as committed to golf as the most fanatical club duffer. He played two or three times a week in season, in fair weather or foul. Right in the middle of a 1921 disarmament conference in Washington, for example, Harding and his secretary of state, Charles Evans Hughes, quietly stole off to play a quick round at Chevy Chase amid a driving November rainstorm. The two were forced to stop after eight holes, not because it was raining so hard—that was no big deal—but because it got too dark to follow the ball.

Then there was the time when Harding was needed to sign a joint congressional resolution terminating the state of war with Imperial Germany. Where was he? Where else? It took his staff almost two hours to get him back from the golf course. When he finally arrived dressed in a jaunty golf outfit, the President read carefully through the vellum document and then signed it. "That's all," he said, as he rose from the table to return to the links.

World War I was officially over.

One Benefit of Golf

How did Harding rationalize all the time he lavished on the game? It was easy. "I may not know everything about being President," he said. "But I do know that a lot of decisions can be made on golf courses."

He was even more compulsive about the game when he went on vacation. The noted advertising man Albert D. Lasker once accompanied the President on a golfing holiday to Florida. They played virtually every course they came across. At the end, Lasker, who was considerably younger than the then 56-year-old Harding, confessed he was completely exhausted. "Thank God the President doesn't skip rope," he said.

Even Harding's Airedale terrier, Laddie Boy, was an important part of his golf. The shaggy, highbred dog was the President's inseparable companion, to such an extent that he sat in on Cabinet meetings and frequently joined his master on the links where, or so one press report would have us believe, he would "bark reproachfully whenever the President stubbed an approach or missed an easy putt."

Laddie Boy was most useful, though, for shagging balls. Harding liked to place an old carpet on the turf outside the Oval Office and drive dozens of golf balls onto the South Lawn. Laddie Boy would scamper after the balls and retrieve as many as he could.

All the practice and all the passion Harding invested in the game, though, produced only mediocre results. That didn't seem to faze him in the slightest. He may have had trouble breaking 100 (his career best was a 92 at Chevy Chase), but his amiability never flagged. "Nobody is more companionable on the links than he," said a frequent partner, Senator Jonathan Bourne Jr. of Oregon. "He's a true lover of the ancient sport. If there does not happen to be a caddie about, he will pick up his bag and carry it cheerfully."

Silver-dollar Tip

A caddie's-eye view of Harding was provided by Shirley Povich, who carried the President's bags as a youngster before going on to become the distinguished and longtime sports editor of *The Washington Post*. Povich was enlisted by McLean to caddie for Harding on some rounds at Friendship. At first, Povich didn't know who Harding was. But he found out quickly enough when McLean said, "Mr. President, I want you to meet Shirley Povich, who's the best caddie in the United States." Povich recalled the drinks that were served on the Friendship course, the "affable" way the President treated him

Swift Swinger: Harding had a habit of rushing his abbreviated backswing and follow-through, which often left him off balance. OHIO HISTORICAL SOCIETY

and Harding's short backswing. "He loved the game," Povich said. "But he wasn't a good golfer. He could shoot 100—sometimes." (The President always gave his caddies a silver dollar as a tip.)

One top sportswriter of the day, Grantland Rice, played with Harding early in his term and reported that the President "knows how to take the breaks of the game as they come and he realizes, which many don't, that bunkers are out there for the express purpose of catching all mistakes. All of which makes him an extremely attractive golf companion, one with dignity minus pretense."

Presidential privilege, moreover, didn't exist for Harding on the golf course. When others in his foursome would offer to concede a short putt or suggest he improve a bad lie, he wouldn't accept the deference to his office. "Forget that I am the President of the United States," he would insist. "I'm Warren Harding, playing with some friends, and I'm going to beat the hell out of them."

That, it must be said, seldom happened, and there seemed to be two key reasons. First, Harding had the unfortunate habit of rushing his shortened, two-thirds swing. Rice observed that the President had "a tendency to start his body in advance of his hands and arms, which comes from a desire to hit a trifle too quickly. . . . If one is a trifle tired or if one's concentration wanders to outside affairs, the advance sway of the body is likely to develop."

The other quality that impeded Harding's progress as a golfer was his relaxed, easygoing approach to the game. Sure, he played to win; he usually had too many bets at stake to do otherwise. Still, he was that rarest of golfers: one who didn't ever let the inevitable frustrations of the game get to him. "He has an utter lack of self-consciousness when he makes a mistake," said one partner. "He does not mind it in the least."

Of course, the President was not without some golfing weapons. He was capable of executing nice short pitches to the green. And his one real strength was his putting. He employed, as William Howard Taft did, the center-shafted Schenectady putter that had been banned for international play but was, nonetheless, widely used in the United States at that time. Sportswriter Rice, who called Harding "a first-class putter," noted that during their round the President "hit the ball firmly throughout. There was no nervous jab or stab, but an even, well-timed follow-through to each putt."

Celebrity Partners

Harding liked to play with celebrities of all kinds. One morning, for instance, he teamed up with Sir Harry Lauder, the Scottish entertainer who had golfed a decade earlier with Taft. The President and Lauder took on McLean and his partner at the Congressional Country Club and, to Harding's delight, licked them by three up and two to go. The President, said Lauder, "was like a schoolboy and he was, to use his own words, 'tickled to death' by the good form we displayed."

Comedian Will Rogers was another presidential golfing guest—though not for long. When they were first introduced, Harding had told Rogers, "This is the first time I ever got to see you without paying for it." But Rogers was soon blacklisted by the White House. It didn't help that he quipped, "Rail splitting produced an immortal President in Abraham Lincoln. But golf, with 29 million courses, hasn't produced even a good A-number-one congressman." What finally made Rogers persona non golf at the White House, though, was one of his vaudeville skits in which Harding was depicted as jabbering away about golf all during a Cabinet meeting. The President was so annoyed when he heard about the skit that he canceled plans to see the show.

Famous Foursome: At the White House before their match were (from left to right) Harding, the eminent sportswriter Grantland Rice, famed humorist Ring Lardner and Under Secretary of State Henry Fletcher. THE AMERICAN GOLFER

Another prominent American humorist, Ring Lardner, figured in the only Harding match of which there is still a public record. Lardner joined Rice as a guest in the round that Rice used as the basis for his observations about the President's game. Under Secretary of State Henry Fletcher rounded out the foursome.

"I believe another rain storm is coming," one of the players remarked as they stood on the first tee at Chevy Chase in April 1921.

"Suppose it does," Harding said. "Why should a rain stop us?"

The conditions weren't good to begin with. The fairways were already soaked from an earlier storm, and a blustery crosswind raked the course. As Rice told it in *The American Golfer* magazine, Harding's "first drive traveled 180 yards down the fairway and he was down in 5 on a 420-yard hole. He went boldly for his 4, overran by five feet, and then, without wasting any extra motions, dropped his second putt into the cup."

The high point of the round for Harding came on the fourth hole, a par 3. His first shot landed on a bare patch "60 yards from the green guarded by an intervening brook," Rice reported. "The case against him here looked to be hopeless. We declined his smiling offer to take a 4 and not play it out. Bad mistake. For he promptly pitched to within eight feet of the cup and sank his putt for a par 3."

Harding and Fletcher held their own against Rice and Lardner on the front nine. "The President obtained a big jump on Mr. Lardner" during the early holes, Rice noted, "forcing the eminent humorist to unfurl his best game in order to escape complete annihilation." Rice indicated, but didn't say outright, that he and Lardner dominated on the back nine. And, perhaps charitably, he didn't report the final results. He said simply that "on the homeward journey the gray sky turned to a deeper darkness around the 15th hole [and] the rain began again at the 17th tee. . . .We should say that under normal conditions [Harding] should be able to average 95."

The four then sought shelter and refreshments in The President's House, a bungalow set aside for the Chief Executive by Chevy

Chase. There, Edmund W. Starling, the Secret Service officer who accompanied Harding on the course as he had Woodrow Wilson, unlocked a desk drawer where several bottles of Scotch and bourbon were stashed—well out of sight of those Prohibition-minded club members. After the drinks were poured, Lardner mentioned that he would appreciate it if the President would appoint him to be the U.S. ambassador to Greece.

When Harding asked why, Lardner's hound-dog face grew even longer.

"Because my wife doesn't like Great Neck," he replied.

Starling, meanwhile, was totting up the bets. While Rice didn't mention it in his article, the gossip later was that he and Lardner had each pocketed almost $100.

Heavy Betting

Harding always had bets going during a match—often a number of them—and it was Starling's job to keep track of them all. The President preferred $6 nassaus ($6 for the front nine, $6 for the back nine and $6 for the match), but he also liked to put an extra fillip of excitement in a match with other side bets. He would lay one with his partner on a low score and then, as the game progressed, he would double up on his wagers, bet on individual holes and even on individual shots as they flew down the fairways.

"He made so many bets that sometimes he was betting against himself," said Starling. "I had to keep accounts and it was a job for a Philadelphia lawyer."

Starling invariably had one last assignment at the end of a round. When the President had finished his drink, he would turn to the Secret Service agent and ask him to "telephone the Duchess and say I'm on my way home."

"The Duchess" was Harding's not altogether affectionate sobriquet for his wife, Florence, a frosty, domineering woman who did her best to keep Harding as close to home as a putt inside the leather. And with good reason, because he did have a wandering eye.

In fact, the golf course was one of the few places where Harding could unshackle himself from the Duchess, which may partially explain why he played so much. She even joined him frequently when he indulged in his other off-hours passion: evenings of poker with his pals. She apparently felt that impure thoughts were more likely to surface around a poker table than on a golf course. But she must have been out of the room during one particularly memorable session. That's when Harding gambled away on a single hand of poker an entire set of White House china dating back to the administration of Benjamin Harrison in the early 1890s.

An Instant Passion

Harding had caught the golf bug almost instantaneously in the autumn of 1917 when he was a U.S. senator from Ohio. He and some fellow senators were visiting Secretary of War John W. Weeks at his home in New England, and Harding tagged along when the group arranged to play at a nearby course. As Senator Frederick Hale of Maine recalled it later, Harding "idly picked up a club and then, like many dubs, he made a remarkable shot. . . . After that, there was no stopping him. We could not head him off even if we had wished to. He insisted on playing right away."

He hardly ever stopped. With his geniality and enthusiasm, Harding was quickly accepted into the so-called Senatorial Foursomes (a select group that, incidentally, also included one popular, non-Senate golfer by the name of Franklin D. Roosevelt, who at that time was serving as assistant secretary of the navy). The group usually played at the Chevy Chase as a twelvesome consisting of three parties of four, with lots of hollering and bantering among the parties. "They are a lot like schoolboys in their rivalry," said one observer.

During one particularly raucous round, for example, some regular Chevy Chase members tried to play through the senatorial group, which was dawdling along somewhat strung out across the course. Senator Joseph T. Robinson of Arkansas took strong exception to this impertinence—so strong that he started a fistfight. Robinson was promptly suspended from the club. He served the suspension with no sense of penitence and then returned to the club as if nothing had happened.

Harding enjoyed those Senate years and harbored no ambitions for the presidency. He told one colleague, Senator James Watson of Indiana, that he was just as happy to stay in the Senate, play some golf and have a good time. But Harding had a number of influential and persistent admirers who pushed him for the White House job. After winning the 1920 Republican presidential nomination at the party's convention in Chicago, Harding was quickly back on the Chevy Chase course. But this time, his new status had gained him a large and intrusive audience of newspaper and newsreel cameramen. Under that pressure, he played as well as he ever did. As a result, he gained that day an undeserved reputation as a reasonably competent golfer.

Photographers were banked around Harding when he stepped up to the first tee. As he described it later, "It is not conducive to good golf to hear camera shutters going and photographers shifting plates. I made a miserable drive off the first tee and didn't do much with my [next shots]. But as I approached the green, I was a few feet off it in the rough.

"I told the men I was going to hole out from there, and I took my putter and did it! I didn't think for a minute I could do it. On the last hole, I did almost identically the same thing."

Harding had, for him, a dream round. With the press hounding his footsteps, he breezed through the first five holes in 5, 5, 5, 3 and 5—only 3 over par for that stretch. He continued to play strongly the rest of the way. In the locker room later, a fellow politician put the presidential race in just the terms Harding could relate to. "Well, I see you got over the first nine pretty well at Chicago," he said to Harding. "I hope you will be as successful in the last nine of the campaign and election."

"Oh," said Harding with a laugh, "I'm always better on the last nine."

Even with the presidency at stake, Harding kept his clubs handy. And in November, when he went home to Marion, Ohio, to vote, he spent most of Election Day not nervously anticipating the returns but golfing in knickers and an old red sweater at the Scioto Country Club in Columbus. After sweeping to victory over the Democrats' James M. Cox in the election, Harding took a month-long vacation with the Duchess that included visits to both the locks and the links in the Panama Canal Zone. There, he played on a pastoral course known as the $8 Million Links because they adjoined the Gatun Locks, which had cost that amount.

A Cheer and a Shrug

Maybe the cows and the sheep grazing on the course disturbed his concentration. Whatever the reason, it was not one of Harding's better golfing days. His shots flew wide into the rough and short into the bunkers. Finally, he nailed one zinger straight down the fairway. His companions gave a cheer, but Harding gave a shrug. "A blind sow," he said glumly, "will find an acorn once in a while."

The President-elect fared better in Florida. A sizable gallery watched him shoot a 101 at the Sea Breeze course in Ormond Beach. Did the gallery put him off? "Not a bit," Harding said. "It helped."

But he learned something about keeping the presidential mouth shut after playing on an atrocious sandy course at a Florida resort. Even though the fairways and greens were in terrible shape (he was forced to putt with a lofted club), Harding made the mistake of pronouncing it "the sportiest golf course in Florida." The resort, understandably, trumpeted those words in its advertisements and, wrote one reporter later, "golfers who took his words seriously and followed him there have not forgiven him."

Did Harding's gusto for golf seem to detract from his suitability for the highest office in the land? On the contrary, golf was apparently seen in some quarters as almost an essential qualification. In a classic instance of championing the trivial, *The New York Times* ran this headline at the top of its front page shortly before Harding took office: "Golfer Sees in Harding's Play Good Omen for Administration."

The article that followed didn't even quote as the authority for this pronouncement some statesman or eminent golf figure. It cited one H. K. Wilcox, an obscure local champion from Middletown, New York. "Mr. Harding," the *Times* solemnly quoted Wilcox as saying, "plays a good game, drives straight, carries through and keeps his eye on the ball—a good omen, I think, for the next four years."

If it were only that simple.

Harding, like every new President, was besieged by office-seekers. But an inventive South Carolina postmaster seeking reappointment came up with a new ploy. He challenged Harding to a round of golf because, he explained, he liked the President's "sporty inclination." The proposed terms of the match: If the postmaster won, he'd keep the job; if Harding won, the postmaster would be looking for work. The President declined the offer, writing that he was unwilling to "have the administration weakened by basing its attitude on my incapacity at golf."

How He Did in Tournaments

But he did accept invitations to play in a few of the tournaments staged by the Washington Newspaper Golf Association (he qualified professionally as the owner of *The Marion Star,* his hometown newspaper in Ohio). The first of the tourneys was held late in the summer of 1921 at the Washington Golf & Country Club in Arlington, Virginia. An attempt was made to rig Harding's handicap so that he would win the event. And the President cooperated by shooting a good score for him—a 97. But this time the photographers got to him. On the 18th green, he was lining up a putt that, if successful, would have given him low net. But just as he began to stroke the ball, he was startled by a clicking shutter and missed the putt. He did earn a prize, however; it was a golf club. And when he presented the winner's trophy, the President said, "It has given me tremendous satisfaction to play with my brother craftsmen this afternoon, and I hope that this tournament is perpetuated."

It was perpetuated, and Harding naturally entered again in 1922—sending along three new one-dollar bills to cover his association dues for three years. "I send this amount," he wrote, "in order to have a clear certification and a closed account for the three years I have to serve. And I hope to be able to show some of the younger fellows how to make a good score." In answer to the question on the application about which golf clubs he belonged to, Harding wrote, "Probably all of them."

The stakes were a bit higher this time when there were separate awards for the lowest gross and net scores. The 12 lowest gross scorers would represent the Washington association in a match against New York newspaper golfers. The President was likely to be available for that confrontation but, unfortunately, he didn't make the cut. At stake for net scores was a large silver trophy that had been donated by Harding's friend McLean of the *Post.* Harding's net score, thanks to the handicap of 22 that he had been given, was good enough for fourth place and a box of golf balls.

The next year the President and the Washington newsmen played their tournament at the Rock Creek public course in Washington, D.C., to baptize that new facility. Harding drove the first ball from the first tee and finished with a 102. Afterward, as golfers are wont to do, he registered some complaints about the course— especially about the condition of the greens. "It was like putting on a corrugated roof," he griped.

But unlike those of most disgruntled golfers, his complaints brought swift action. A crew from the Department of Agriculture was soon on the scene, and, according to one report, "the course became a veritable paradise for golfers [with its] velvety greens."

All his publicized play brought Harding little of the grief that Taft had caught about his constant golfing. To be sure, there was some negative feedback, like the report that when a movie house ran a newsreel of the President golfing, "there was not a hand clap save one." But *The American Golfer* announced that "Mr. Harding placed the stamp of approval on the game. Anyone who could find

the time and money to indulge on public or private courses did so."
And *The New York Times,* ever a defender of Harding's golf, rallied
with these words of support after the President played 36 holes in
one day while vacationing in Florida during the winter of 1923:
"After all, 36 holes a day is a very good preparation for the 10 times
that number of problems he will have to deal with when he resumes
the day's grind at Washington." Harding couldn't have put it more
generously himself.

The Final Round

The President, however, didn't have much more golf to play or
grind to endure. Although he was only 57, he was aging noticeably.
His heart was failing, and within a few months he often grew too
tired to play more than 11 or 12 holes in a round.

*Last Shot: An ailing Harding played his final round in Vancouver, Canada. He is
shown putting out on the 18th green one week before he died from a cerebral hemorrhage.*
OHIO HISTORICAL SOCIETY

One afternoon he asked Starling of the Secret Service, "Colonel, why after playing 11 or 12 holes do I drag my feet and feel so tired?"

"You're working too hard," Starling replied. "You need a vacation. Why don't you confine your game to nine holes until you rest up?"

"Hell," Harding snapped, "if I can't play 18 holes I won't play at all."

Despite his precarious health, the President embarked on a strenuous, cross-country campaign by rail to rally support for the World Court and other administration causes—much as President Wilson had tried, and failed, to do for the League of Nations just four years earlier. Harding even visited Alaska, the first President to do that.

He played golf for the last time on his way back from Alaska at a stopover in Vancouver, Canada. He made it through the first six holes, but then his strength waned. Out of sight of the public and the press, he rested and then cut over to finish up with the 17th and 18th holes so there would be no suspicion about his condition.

Harding died of a cerebral hemorrhage one week later in San Francisco. That city saluted his memory by naming a public golf course in honor of this singularly zestful golfing President.

PLAYING WITH THE PROS

W arren Harding's modest golf skills didn't prevent him from seeking all types of golf partners—the more proficient, the better. Two of history's greatest golfers, Gene Sarazen and Walter Hagen, were frequent visitors to the White House as well as occasional golfing partners during Harding's term.

During one round, the President asked if there was some favor he could do for Hagen.

A Special Keepsake: After a round with Gene Sarazen (left), Harding requested and received the professional's driver.

AP/WIDE WORLD PHOTOS

"It's like this, Mr. President," Hagen replied. "You know I have a reputation for being late to my golf engagements. Sometimes I drive too fast [in order to be on time]. Now one of those deputy Secret Service badges you sometimes give out would do me a heap of good with the speed cops."

Hagen got his badge.

But Harding, too, got something. He had been quite taken with Sarazen's driver and, after the round, asked if he could have it. "What can you say when the President asks for your club?" mused Sarazen after he turned over the driver.

Harding, moreover, was not above summoning some strong reinforcements when the golfing situation seemed to call for it. For instance, at one point he suffered a string of distressing losses to Senator Frank Kellogg of Minnesota and Under Secretary of State Henry Fletcher.

So Harding rolled in the heavy artillery in the form of Chick Evans, who had been the first player to capture the U.S. Amateur and U.S. Open titles in one year (1916) and whose game was so incredibly sound that he was able to compete in every U.S. Amateur Championship between 1907 and 1962. In the ensuing match, Kellogg and Fletcher got blown away—thanks to Evans—and the President had his vengeance.

CHAPTER 5

CALVIN COOLIDGE

Parsimony, Not Par

"Caddie," the golfer asked as he took some warm-up swings, "are you any good at finding lost balls?"

"Best around, sir," the caddie replied.

"Find one, then, and let's get started."

That joke wasn't aimed directly at Calvin Coolidge, but it might just as well have been. Coolidge was to stinginess what Bobby Jones was to championship golf in the 1920s; in other words, he pretty much defined it. This was a President who was such a tightwad that he refused to permit 21-gun salutes in his honor because, he grumbled, "it costs money to fire so many guns."

His Yankee sense of thrift extended, predictably, to the golf links. There was the time, for example, when Coolidge was playing with Freddie McLeod, a top Washington professional. At one point in the round, the President took an awkward swipe at the ball and shattered the wooden shaft of his club when it struck the ground. He turned to McLeod and asked anxiously, "Freddie, that can be fixed, can't it?" Unfortunately, it couldn't, to Coolidge's great dismay.

Of all the golfing Presidents, Coolidge was the most indifferent player as well as the most miserly one. He did, to be sure,

recognize that there were some benefits attached to the game. "I think it is a fine method of relaxation for men in business life," he said. But then he quickly added that "like everything else which is an outside enterprise, it can undoubtedly be carried to excess." The word *excess,* in his case, could clearly be translated to mean "excessive cost."

The expense of golf, in fact, was one reason Coolidge almost always cited to explain why he didn't play the game more often, even when he was earning a then lordly salary of $75,000 a year as President from 1923 to 1929 and salting away much of it. But there may have been another reason for his attitude: He seemed to have little aptitude for golf—or for any other sport, for that matter.

It was ironic. Here the country was in the 1920s experiencing its first great—perhaps its greatest—sports boom. Such figures as Babe Ruth in baseball, Red Grange in football, Jack Dempsey in boxing, Bill Tilden in tennis and Jones in golf were assuming a mythic stature. Golf, like many sports, was flourishing at the grass-roots level, and the game had, in the process, captivated much of Congress. Yet at 1600 Pennsylvania Avenue, the nation's leader was usually getting his exercise by doing nothing more athletic than ambling out for a morning stroll or riding a mechanical hobby horse.

It probably wouldn't have mattered much, in terms of golf at the White House, if Coolidge had lost the 1924 national election (15 months after succeeding Warren G. Harding) and Democrat John W. Davis had become President instead. Davis, a Wall Street lawyer, was described as a "bad though companionable" golfer, and he confessed that rainy Sundays were his favorite days because then, "Thank God, I don't have to play golf."

Incongruous Sight

But Coolidge won the election comfortably, and on those occasions when he did golf, he often selected the course that had also been favored by Harding (although they evidently never shared a round there or anywhere else). The setting was the private links of Edward B. McLean of *The Washington Post* at his Friendship estate. Coolidge was still the Vice President under Harding when he was invited to Friendship for the first time by McLean's wife, Evalyn, the daughter of a gold-mining king and owner of that star-crossed gem, the Hope diamond. Coolidge showed up wearing a suit jacket and high-waisted trousers that were held up by suspenders. He presented an incongruous sight traipsing along beside his partners, who were fashionably attired in plus-fours and bright argyle-patterned socks.

To make things easy for Coolidge, the golfers started out on one of Friendship's shorter holes, a 130-yarder. Coolidge, the only President who played left-handed, removed his jacket and selected an iron. He pecked away at the ball repeatedly down the fairway and eventually took 11 blows to reach the green. Obviously, Coolidge was among the many for whom golf was, and is, a struggle.

Some speculated that he hit only short distances in order to avoid the unbearable prospect of losing a ball. In that respect, he was much like the Scotsman of legend who played the links at North Berwick for 25 years with the same ball. He finally decided the time had come to buy a new one, walked into the North Berwick pro shop and announced sourly, "Weel, here I am ageen."

Unfortunately, Coolidge's game didn't improve much with play and neither did his wardrobe. As President, he once showed up for a match wearing a white canvas hat, no coat, a pair of ragged trousers and, instead of golf shoes, a pair of ankle-high gym sneakers. Whatever fashion statement he was making was as lost on his partners as it had been at McLean's Friendship course. (McLean, a golf host to two Presidents, would meet a wretched end. He became ensnared in the Teapot Dome scandal, lost control of the *Post,* battled his wife in the courts and in 1933 was declared insane.)

Gradually, whatever enthusiasm the President had for the game began to dissipate. "You have to dress for golf," he groused. "Then you have to drive out to some club. . . . It takes three hours to play a round, then you have to undress, take a shower, dress again and drive back. . . . Callers at the White House might wonder why the President wasn't on the job."

The excuse was a lame one. William Howard Taft, of course, had caught some abuse for his love of golf earlier in the century. But, as Coolidge well knew, Harding—in the freewheeling atmosphere of the 1920s—had not suffered for his habitual and well-advertised play. Indeed, far from escaping criticism for playing too much golf, Coolidge took some raps for playing too little. After he vacationed in Sioux Falls, South Dakota, in 1927, for instance, *The American Golfer* lamented that "it was too bad the Chief Executive [was not among those] who are given to walloping golf balls over the thousands of courses throughout the country. For Sioux Falls was equipped and ready to lead him to the scenes of activities of this kind that must surely have pleased him, had he been only of the golfing clan."

Beyond that, much of official Washington had, by then, been smitten by the game. Vice President Charles G. Dawes, Secretary of State Frank Kellogg and a number of others in Coolidge's inner circle were confirmed golfers. (Will Rogers had returned from his White House banishment under Harding, and when Coolidge asked the celebrated wit to "tell me the latest jokes," Rogers responded, "I don't have to. You've appointed them.")

Up on Capitol Hill, *The American Golfer* reported, "No Congressman today would think of foregoing his golf for fear of public disfavor. Golf bags in the Senate and House office buildings are as common as brief cases, lame ducks and lobbyists. Even the House and Senate pages turn out players of ability." Some congressional foursomes arrived at the Potomac Park course as early as 5 A.M. Luckier ones used the private, nine-hole course that had been installed by Senator Millard E. Tydings at his nearby Maryland estate.

The corridors of Congress, meanwhile, buzzed excitedly during this period with a rumor that Bobby Jones might be joining the House to replace a Georgia representative who had recently passed away. The legislators were eager to receive him, but Jones stayed out of politics. Still, observed *The American Golfer,* "If Jones ever does come to Congress, he will not lack for golfing competition."

Slow Start

Coolidge, whom political commentator H. L. Mencken whimsically termed "the greatest man ever to come out of Plymouth, Vermont," had first golfed in 1905 on his honeymoon in Montreal. The game failed to attract him then, however, and even though he didn't pursue it again for years, he did encourage his two sons to take it up while the family belonged to the Belmont Springs Country Club in suburban Boston before moving to Washington. Calvin junior preferred tennis, though, and that led to the White House's greatest sports-related tragedy. While playing one day on the White House tennis court in sneakers without socks, 16-year-old Calvin developed an inflamed blister on one of his toes. He got the

First Ladies as Golf Fans: Grace Coolidge (left) and Florence Harding took in the 1921 U.S. Open at the Columbia Country Club in Chevy Chase, Maryland. U.S. GOLF ASSOCIATION

best medical attention available at that time but, nonetheless, he died from blood poisoning within days. "When he went," his father wrote later, "the power and the glory of the Presidency went with him."

Coolidge himself never played tennis, or much of anything else. He didn't swim, sail, hunt, bowl, ride horseback or play billiards. When asked if he had taken some part in sports while in college at Amherst, he replied, "Yes, I did, an important part." He paused and then added dryly, "I held the stakes."

As President, Coolidge's two main sources of exercise were his morning walks, which really amounted to leisurely window-shopping excursions around the White House neighborhood, and his rides on his mechanical horse. It had been a gift, and the first time he mounted it he was, characteristically, attired in a hat and a business suit. The motions of the contraption so startled him that he lost his hat and almost his seat. He eventually mastered the art of staying aboard, although an electrician's mate from a local navy yard had to make frequent house calls because the President, as the seaman explained it, "don't know how to change the gaits."

Coolidge's wife, Grace, was far more active. She didn't golf, but she took longer and much brisker walks than he did—striding out for five or six miles each day. She was an avid horsewoman until the President put a stop to it ("Horseback riding," he claimed, "keeps your feet too far from the ground"). She was also a die-hard baseball fan, to such a degree that she was known as the First Lady of Baseball and often sat in the Washington Senators' dugout when she attended their games. The President didn't share, in the slightest, this preoccupation with baseball. The nation got some insight into his knowledge of it when he threw out the first ball at the Senators' opening game in 1924 and informed reporters that "Babe Ruth made a big mistake when he gave up pitching."

Although Coolidge was only a sometime golfer, he and Grace got top billing at the grandest golfing occasion in Washington during their years in the White House. It was the opening in 1924 of the Congressional Country Club in Bethesda, Maryland. The original $1,000 memberships were bought by the likes of the John D. Rockefellers (senior and junior), Vincent Astor, Harvey S. Firestone, various du Ponts and, for some reason, Charlie Chaplin.

"President and Diplomats Attend Brilliant Opening of Congressional Club," read the headline in *The Washington Post* the next day. When the Coolidges arrived, the accompanying story reported, "Hundreds of flares were set off in different parts of the grounds to welcome them. The Marine Band, in dress uniform, was drawn up before the clubhouse and played a march" as the Coolidges entered.

They mingled briefly with 7,000 other guests, but there was little pressing of the flesh. The President followed his new policy of not shaking hands unless it was absolutely required of him. After they were shown around the clubhouse, the Coolidges went to the Presidential Suite, where they had a dinner that featured a main course of steak and french fries (that's what Coolidge had asked for and that's what was served). The Presidential Suite, club publicity promised, "would be kept ever in readiness for occupancy by the President of the United States." The promise lasted for all of six years. Then the club started renting the room out for $25 a day, and later it was converted into a tournament office.

Coolidge didn't stay at the party for long; he insisted on nine hours of sleep per night. But he departed with an assurance that he was "Congressional's distinguished Honorary Life Member." That must have particularly pleased him because it didn't cost him a nickel. But he apparently never used the membership—certainly not after he retired from the presidency. One of the few personal items that the niggardly New Englander left behind in the White House was his set of golf clubs.

WHAT DID COOLIDGE HAVE IN COMMON WITH BEN HOGAN?

He may have been the least talented of presidential golfers, but Calvin Coolidge had one quality in common with one of the game's greatest players. Like Ben Hogan, he was a man of few words.

Pro star Jimmy Demaret once revealed what it was like to play with Hogan when he was asked what Hogan had said during a round. "Nothing," Demaret said, "except, 'You're away.'"

Ben Hogan: Just two words.

AP/WIDE WORLD PHOTOS

Similarly, a woman seated next to Coolidge during a White House dinner gushed that she had bet a friend she could get the President to say more than two words.

Silent Cal studied her for a moment and then said, "You lose."

CHAPTER 6

FRANKLIN D. ROOSEVELT

Yes, He Did Play Golf

In the spring of 1890, financier James Roosevelt returned from a trip to southern France with his family and what was, at that time, some uncommon cargo: a hefty, wooden box containing an assortment of golf clubs. He had just learned the game and was so infatuated with it that he wanted to introduce it to his circle of patrician friends at home.

His eight-year-old son, Franklin, almost certainly looked on—although family chronicles don't say so for sure—as Roosevelt laid out a six-hole course in the fields around the family's estate in Hyde Park, New York. There, Roosevelt and other members of the local landed gentry were soon whiling away their weekend afternoons whacking gutta-percha balls around the quiet pastures. One of those pioneering U.S. golfers was Colonel Archibald Rogers, an associate of John D. Rockefeller's. Rogers picked the game up so quickly that he was a top contender when the first U.S. Amateur championship was played a few years later at the Newport Country Club in Rhode Island.

Golf and golfers, thus, were a part of Franklin D. Roosevelt's world almost from the game's beginnings in the United States. And when he took up the sport himself in his teenage years, he found

A Driving Force: Roosevelt was recognized as "one of the longest driving amateurs" in the Washington area during World War I. But he had a swing that produced length rather than accuracy. COURTESY, THE FRANKLIN D. ROOSEVELT LIBRARY

that he had the physical tools to play it quite well. No less an authority than Walter Camp, the legendary football coach and early fitness guru, once described the young Roosevelt as "a beautifully built man with the long muscles of the athlete." That, combined with a true zeal for the game, made him a most accomplished player for his day—or any other.

Indeed, the history of the Congressional Country Club in Bethesda, Maryland, notes that while serving in the Woodrow Wilson administration during World War I, Roosevelt was "one of the longest driving amateurs in the area." His great strength meant that even playing out of the rough caused him little difficulty. That was important since photographs taken at the time reveal a powerful—almost too powerful—swing, since it produced a follow-through designed for length rather than accuracy. He was, nonetheless, still able to score consistently in the high 80s and, on one exhilarating occasion, to win his club championship.

The Unluckiest of All

More than a century ago, golfer-historian Horace Hutchinson observed that all golfers consider themselves unlucky. But of all the U.S. Presidents who've played the game, Roosevelt's misfortune was the most devastating. Poliomyelitis paralyzed him from the waist down at age 39, crippling him cruelly for life and ending his golfing days a dozen years before he reached the White House in 1933. Surely the most poignant words ever uttered about presidential golf were these by Roosevelt's wife, Eleanor: "Golf was the game that Franklin enjoyed above all others. . . . After he was stricken with polio, the one word that he never said again was golf."

Poignant, perhaps, but not entirely accurate. As it happened, Roosevelt continued his interest in the game after he was stricken. Among other things, he oversaw the design and construction of an innovative nine-hole course, gleefully heckled friends on the few occasions when he could accompany them on a round and, with his public works programs, did more for the municipal-course player than any other U.S. President to this day.

Roosevelt started out in golf, not on his father's homemade course at Hyde Park, but at the family's summer retreat on Campobello Island, which lies two miles off the coast of Maine in the

Canadian province of New Brunswick. One day while he was in his early teens and out sailing, a dense fog forced him to seek refuge with some friends. During the visit, they showed him the rudiments of golf, and he returned home completely gung-ho about the game. So much so that he followed his father's example and promptly created a makeshift course of his own on the family's four acres at Campobello.

Young Roosevelt's golf clubs accompanied him to boarding school at Groton, north of Boston, and later to college at Harvard. He had, undeniably, a knack for the game. During his senior year at Groton, he wrote his parents to tell them proudly, "I broke my record on the links yesterday, doing 41, which is within two strokes of the record of the course." His only other athletic achievement of note at Groton occurred in an event called the high kick, in which a contestant used a swift scissors motion with the legs to reach as high as he could with one foot. Roosevelt set a school record of seven feet, three and one-half inches. (It's a talent that would seem

Early Achievements:
In boarding school at
Groton, Roosevelt shot a
41 for nine holes (two
short of the course record)
in 1899. After grad-
uation from Harvard, he
won his club championship.
COURTESY, THE FRANKLIN D.
ROOSEVELT LIBRARY

to be absolutely irrelevant to golf. But who knows? Sam Snead was another who excelled at the maneuver, so much so that he could still kick the top of a door frame when he was nearly 70.)

A formal golf club, meanwhile, had been established at Campobello with James Roosevelt serving as its president. The dues for the 77 members were five dollars a year. For that, they got a nine-hole course that was described as "rough and difficult [with] not too smooth greens." The course, moreover, also featured some picturesque, if obstinate, hazards: the sheep that grazed there. Nonetheless, FDR (he used the acronym even then) captured his first golf prize on its course at age 16 in competition against older players. The trick, he said, was to "simply aim well over the [sheeps'] heads, shut your eyes and hope for the best." Roosevelt's mother, Sara, wrote years later that "Franklin won . . . but it is difficult now to remember whether the score was recorded in strokes or sheep."

The trophy, however, wasn't engraved fast enough to suit young Roosevelt. So he got on his parents' case about it, writing from Groton at one point to remind them to have "the man who is marking my golf cup to send it up here as I would like to keep it on the mantelpiece in our room."

Winter Wager

Even in those years, Roosevelt was proud of his power off the tee. There's the story, which may be apocryphal, of the time he bet a classmate that he could drive a golf ball more than 300 yards. And he won the bet. But he did it by waiting until winter and then hitting the ball onto a frozen pond.

The young man's golfing skills, maturity and jaunty self-assurance were such, moreover, that the Campobello club named him its secretary/treasurer when he was all of 18 and still at Groton. The post involved all the thankless tasks that have burdened golf committeemen almost since the first ball was struck—from overseeing the course to dunning members for dues. Even Roosevelt's doting mother thought he was too young for the job. But he accepted it anyway, explaining to her, "I don't mind the work, and

I don't mind the slanders of our neighbors, and I intend to hand the position back with the club in as good condition as when I take it." When his mother then volunteered to help him with the paperwork, he gently declined the offer and handled it all himself.

It was golf, as a result, that gave Roosevelt his first taste of administrative responsibilities. The schoolboy seemed to cope with them admirably. He organized some improvements at the club—such as enlarging several of the course's tees and greens. And he had handsome new scorecards, invitation cards and stationery printed. He also made his debut as a public speaker when he addressed the membership about the proper use of the course. The talk went so well that, afterward, he won congratulations from another summer Campobello resident, Justice Horace Gray of the U.S. Supreme Court.

But after serving for one year, Roosevelt resigned the club post following his father's death from heart disease in 1900. He and his mother found the prospect of returning to Campobello the next summer without James Roosevelt too painful; they sailed to Europe instead.

A Big Moment

FDR was back at Campobello in the summer of 1904, after graduating from Harvard, for perhaps his greatest golfing moment. He won the Campobello Golf Club championship and, with it, one leg on a handsome silver cup that would go to the first member to take the title three years in a row.

Neither Roosevelt, nor anyone else for that matter, would ever manage to accomplish that. The club was soon dissolved, done in by competition from a tonier facility built about 15 miles away by the Canadian Pacific Railroad. (As President some 40 years later, though, Roosevelt would learn that the cherished silver cup, orphaned by the Campobello club, still existed. It had been donated by a former Campobello member to the Jefferson Islands Club, a Washington organization that listed among its officers such heavy political hitters as

House Speaker Sam Rayburn, Vice-President-to-be Alben W. Barkley and presidential confidante Bernard M. Baruch.)

But the end of the Campobello club by no means ended Roosevelt's golf, of course. By the next spring, he was playing most of his golf in Europe where he and Eleanor were spending their honeymoon. Roosevelt tested many famous courses, including the most famous of them all: St. Andrews in Scotland. Eleanor, for her part, got the first inkling that she was fated to become a golf widow—until polio struck FDR down 16 years later.

Eleanor Tries Golf

Eleanor tried gamely to escape that destiny by secretly taking golf lessons. "Because my husband played golf," she wrote in a memoir, "I made a valiant effort one year to practice every day, trying to learn how to play." As the First Lady and then as head of the United Nations Commission on Human Rights years later, Eleanor would become a beloved and world-renowned humanitarian. But she had no aptitude for golf. According to one of her sons, she even lacked the coordination to drive an automobile competently. So the outcome was probably inevitable when, as she told it, "after days of practice I went out [golfing] with my husband one day. After watching me for a few minutes, he remarked he thought that I might just as well give it up! . . . I never again attempted anything but walking with my husband."

Roosevelt's most active golfing years came after he went to Washington in 1913 to serve as assistant secretary of the navy in the Wilson administration. His golf sticks were rarely idle. During the first summer, for instance, he wrote his mother, saying, "I'm off at 4 P.M. to play golf. Tomorrow also I am to golf, so you will see that I'm taking good care of myself." In fact, his son Elliott said that "during his seven years in the Navy Department, FDR played golf almost every time he could spare several hours away from the office."

Often, Roosevelt would hop a trolley to ride from the old State, War and Navy Building on Pennsylvania Avenue out to the course of the Chevy Chase Club in Maryland. His game, plus his infectious charm and enthusiasm, made him a popular companion among the regulars at the club. He was one of the few outsiders admitted to the exclusive coterie known as the Senatorial Foursomes. Every now and then he was paired with Warren G. Harding, then a U.S. senator from Ohio. As best it can be determined, it was the first time that two U.S. Presidents—past, present or future—played golf together. Although Roosevelt was a favorite of Wilson's, the President was such a reclusive golfer that the two apparently never shared a round.

For some of the senatorial matches, Roosevelt asked his eldest son, James, to act as his caddie. "Father decided I should earn my allowance—25 cents a week—by caddieing for him," the son recalled in his memoir about FDR. "He played with various men in public life. Several times I caddied for Father when his partner was Harding. All I remember about Harding was that he seemed amiable and that Father enjoyed golfing with him."

Roosevelt was one of those who played golf religiously—in other words, every Sunday. These sessions at Chevy Chase delighted James, he said, "because I got to skip church occasionally in favor of the golf course. I loved it and would have foregone my allowance for the privilege." The Sunday rounds, though, didn't wash at all well with Eleanor, who, not unlike countless other golf widows, complained that her husband was "leaving me to take the children to church."

But Roosevelt wasn't as indifferent to his wife as it may have appeared. The only recorded slump that he endured in golf coincided, in 1918, with a rocky phase in his marriage. Suddenly, there was a sharp deterioration in his scores. Livingston Davis, an old friend who had been playing with him since they were classmates at Harvard, was one of those who noticed it. He was puzzled to find that, for no apparent reason, he was winning every match. "Never saw FD [sic] play so poorly," Davis noted in his diary after one round. A marital truce was eventually reached, and Roosevelt's game recuperated.

By 1920, Roosevelt was James M. Cox's vice presidential running mate on the Democratic national ticket that opposed his onetime golfing crony, Harding. The Republican nominee didn't let the campaign interrupt his golf, of course, and neither did Roosevelt. After a luncheon speech in Billings, Montana, for instance, he asked, "Do you have a golf course hereabouts?"

He was informed that they did but also that it was raining heavily. Did he wish to play in the rain?

"Sure!" Roosevelt exclaimed. So they assembled a foursome and played nine holes in the downpour.

How did he do? "I don't remember his score," J. B. Arnold, his partner, said later. "But I do recall he played a fine game."

It was also among his last.

The next summer at Campobello, Roosevelt fell victim to polio. At first he refused to accept his paralysis and talked confidently of recovery—even of resuming golf. He wrote to the Dutchess Golf & Country Club near his Hyde Park home in 1923, for example, asking to be transferred from an active to an inactive membership. In his letter he said, "I am still on crutches and cannot possibly play golf for a year or two."

He also corresponded with Wilson, who lay stricken by a stroke in Washington. "I am indeed delighted to hear you are getting well so fast and so confidently," Wilson wrote him, "and I shall try to be generous enough not to envy you." Later, word was sent to Roosevelt that the two invalids were now engaged in a race to see which one would be able to return to the golf course first.

A New Kind of Course

FDR eventually put his hopes in the restorative powers of the waters at Warm Springs, Georgia, where he had found encouraging—if short-lived—relief from his affliction. In 1926 he bought the dilapidated old spa there and embarked on an ambitious program to create an advanced center for the treatment of polio victims alongside a resort for well-heeled vacationers.

Wistful Reminder: A golf ball (lower left) was perched on his desk in the Oval Office when Roosevelt signed the declaration of war against Japan on December 8, 1941.
UPI/BETTMANN

To lure them, he talked of such attractions as a quail-shooting preserve, a "magnificent" clubhouse and two 18-hole golf courses.

He never got those 36 holes, but he did manage nine. And they comprised one of the world's most unusual golf courses—one fashioned so that polio sufferers could enjoy the game along with everyone else. With Roosevelt involved in every step of the design and construction, the course was built to accommodate a network of roads and specially reinforced bridges. They permitted those polio victims who could walk short distances to play by driving automobiles around the course. Others, like Roosevelt, who couldn't walk at all but liked to watch, could at least motor along to follow the action.

After the course opened, Roosevelt would take his secretary, Missy LeHand, or a pretty nurse along as he shouted bawdy advice to the players and took occasional sips from a silver pitcher of martinis to salute the good shots—and the bad.

When he won the White House a few years later, Roosevelt's impairment made him the only golfing President who never played while occupying that office. But many of his top lieutenants were golfers, and they were frequently the objects of presidential gibes.

A friend once wrote the President about an eagle 2 that an aide, Stephen Early, had scored in a local club tournament. The President replied that Early had told him about the eagle but that he had his doubts about its legitimacy: "Steve came back most unexpectedly with money in his pocket and with a tall tale about how somebody's ball knocked his in a cup. We still think he was in his cups! The FBI is investigating."

On another occasion, Guy Mason, the commissioner of the District of Columbia, wrote Roosevelt to ask if Early and two other White House staffers could be called golfing "gentlemen." The President responded, "In the first place, I did not know that any one of the three could be classified as a golfer." But he offered to visit the Burning Tree Club in Bethesda, Maryland, "some Sunday morning and . . . then drive around the course a bit to see for myself just how the Unholy Three conduct themselves on tee, fairway and green."

In 1940, Roosevelt donated to Burning Tree the brassie he had used in Washington from 1913 to 1920. He added one caveat, however: "Don't let anyone try to use it. Being nearly 30 years old, it might disintegrate." No one ever has used it. Since that day it has stood on display at Burning Tree alongside clubs donated by other Presidents (see chapter 1).

In the end, Roosevelt made his most significant contribution to the game of golf—one that's almost completely unrecognized—with the public works programs that his administration devised to help the nation survive the Depression. The Roosevelt policies resulted in, among other things, the construction of more than 250 new municipal courses that opened up the game to thousands upon thousands of new players.

"Roosevelt has done much to change the complexion of U.S. golf," wrote newspaperman Bob Considine of the usually anti-Roosevelt Hearst chain in 1940. "The untold hundreds of thousands of dollars appropriated to enable American cities to build courses has resulted in the tapping of . . . a different type of Average Player. He is John Doe, successor to John Dough." Considine added that "the greenskeepers, now practically a division of Mr. Roosevelt's Department of Agriculture, have made amazing strides in developing new and tougher grasses, and truer greens, to encourage the newcomer. . . .

"Roosevelt for the Vardon Trophy!"

LOWELL THOMAS PROMISED "A LOT OF LAUGHS"

W hen Franklin D. Roosevelt was at the family's estate in Hyde Park, New York, one of his nearby acquaintances was Lowell Thomas, the celebrated adventurer and doyen of American

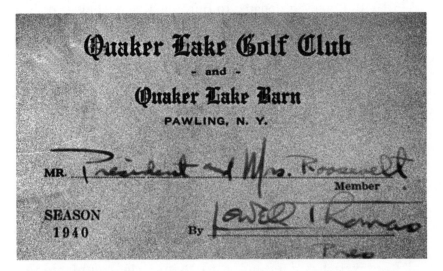

Membership Card: It was, sadly, never used. COURTESY, THE FRANKLIN D. ROOSEVELT LIBRARY

newscasters. Thomas was also the president of his local golf club, Quaker Lake, in Pawling, New York.

In July 1940, he issued and signed a Quaker Lake membership card for President and Mrs. Roosevelt. He invited them to visit the club when, he wrote, "you happen to have a weekend at Hyde Park and feel the need of an antidote and a lot of laughs." But World War II had begun in Europe, so FDR replied, "I fear the uncertainty of the times will not permit a definite commitment."

Thomas would later build a private golf course on his Pawling estate with design input from the noted architect Robert Trent Jones. The course, which Thomas named the Hammersley Hill Golf and Hunt Club, had 18 tees and nine greens. Each of the greens had two sets of cups; one was the standard four-and-one-quarter-inch size and the other was cut at eight inches. The larger cups were installed at the suggestion of Gene Sarazen, who contended that golf would be a more enjoyable game if it provided easier putting targets.

Roosevelt never got to see this unique course. But many other luminaries got a chance to try it, including two Presidents: Dwight D. Eisenhower and Richard M. Nixon.

CHAPTER 7

DWIGHT D. EISENHOWER
Two Terms on the Golf Course

N o other U.S. President has been so identified with golf as Dwight D. Eisenhower. But then, no other President has ever been quite so consumed by the game. How far gone was Ike on golf? Consider the following random slices from life at the White House during his eight presidential years (1953 to 1961):

- The first thing Eisenhower did after dressing each morning was to reach for a golf club he had at the ready and start swinging it to limber up a bit. Did he leave the club behind? Perish the thought. He would take it along to swing periodically during the day as he prowled the halls of the Executive Mansion.
- At the end of his work day, the President would usually slip into his golf shoes and step out of the Oval Office to work on his game. He would practice his iron shots on the South Lawn and hone his putting stroke on a green that had been specially installed for him.
- One day, a visitor to the White House noticed that the President was wearing a bandage on his left wrist. When Eisenhower explained that he had a mild arthritic condition, the visitor

A World-Class Golf Fanatic: During his White House years, Eisenhower played no fewer than 800 rounds of golf. UPI/BETTMANN

expressed relief that it wasn't anything serious. "I should say it is serious," the President exclaimed indignantly. "It means that I can't play golf!"

- Eisenhower awoke one Saturday to discover that a rainstorm threatened to wash out his scheduled golf game. He kept peering out the window of the Oval Office during the morning to see if the downpour was letting up. When it didn't, he stood at the window and told his secretary mournfully, "Sometimes I feel so sorry for myself I could cry!"

- A reporter, who interviewed Eisenhower while he was recovering from his heart attack, began by inquiring how the President was feeling. "Pretty well, pretty well," Ike replied, "but I'm having trouble getting around on the ball."

- In 1960, the Eisenhower administration suffered perhaps its most embarrassing moments after the Soviets discovered that a top-secret American U-2 plane was spying on them and shot the aircraft down. At the height of the ensuing crisis, Soviet leader Nikita Khrushchev noted pointedly that "there is a strained situation, after all, and yet the President has chosen to go off to his golf course."

Eisenhower was, in short, a world-class golf fanatic. Clifford Roberts encountered more than a few of them in his days as the co-founder, with Bobby Jones, of the Augusta National Golf Club in Georgia and as the longtime chairman of its Masters tournament. But Roberts maintained that Ike, a member of the club, "was the most enthusiastic golfer I ever knew. He was worse than Arnold Palmer in changing his equipment and style."

The names of this President and that golf professional are, in fact, forever linked in golfing lore. They made an improbable pair, the soldier-statesman and the greenskeeper's son, but together Eisenhower and Palmer were widely considered the catalysts of the golf boom of the 1950s and early 1960s—Palmer, with his charismatic, charge-from-behind style of play, seen on the young medium of television, and Eisenhower, with the high visibility he lent the game as an immensely popular President. Ike, according to Sam Snead, was "the greatest thing that ever happened to the game." He gave it, in the words of one commentator, "the White Housekeeping seal of approval."

Airing Out the War Room

But Eisenhower's incessant play brought with it flak from critics and razzing from comedians. One joke at the time had the President and his golfing party asking the foursome ahead of them if they could play through.

"What's your hurry?" they were asked.

"The Russians have just bombed New York," came the reply.

But Ike, ignoring all the barbs and quips, unabashedly played on. "You have to let a little air into the war room now and then," the former five-star General liked to say by way of explaining how the game refreshed him. So he was out on the links two or three

*Historic Pairing:
An engrossed Arnold
Palmer watched as
Eisenhower, his partner
in a charity exhibition,
rolled in a 45-foot putt.*
AP/WIDE WORLD PHOTOS

times a week when he was in Washington (at the Burning Tree
Club in Bethesda, Maryland) and once or twice daily when he was
on holiday (at Augusta National). Nor, in the end, was his compul-
sion for golf a political liability. On the contrary, it seemed to help
in Eisenhower's reelection campaign of 1956.

The White House used claims of his robust play at Augusta
National and other courses in 1956 as proof that—after two serious illnesses—he was fit enough to serve a second term in the
White House. There were some who whimsically championed
another candidate. Bumper stickers appeared during the campaign
that exclaimed, "Ben Hogan for President. If We've Got to Have a
Golfer in the White House, Let's Have a Good One."

In assessing his game, Eisenhower termed himself an "ordinary
duffer." But he was, in reality, somewhat better than that. His
handicap ranged between 14 and 18, and he broke 80 at least three
times—posting 79s at Burning Tree, Augusta National and the

Gettysburg Country Club in Pennsylvania. If golfers drive for show but putt for dough, then it could be said that Eisenhower was a fine showman—but one who was fairly often in debt. Putting, year in and year out, was the weakest part of his game. Still, as his good friend Bobby Jones observed, "He can make enough good shots to have fun."

Ike, moreover, certainly kept better golfing company than any ordinary duffer. A President can have his choice of golfing companions, of course, and Eisenhower mined that rich perk by playing with a long series of big names—everyone from captains of industry to legends of show business to giants of professional golf.

Comedian Bob Hope was one occasional partner, and he, naturally, milked his rounds with the President for a constant stream of one-liners. "Ike plays like a General," Hope quipped. "Every time he strokes a putt, he snaps to attention and barks, 'Fall in.'" Hope also remarked that "playing golf with Ike is very handy. If you hit a ball into the rough and it stops near a tree, the tree suddenly becomes a Secret Service man and moves away."

Among the top pros Eisenhower played with were such illustrious figures as Palmer, Snead, Hogan, Byron Nelson and Cary Middlecoff. "The President shoots a nice game," said Hogan, "for a man whose job doesn't give him much chance to play or practice." (If Hogan had only known how intensely Ike did both!) Middlecoff declared that "the President shoots a lot better golf than I thought he would. He can belt one [nicely] off the tee and knock it a pretty good chunk from the fairway . . . [and] he chips exceptionally well."

Snead was not quite so generous. He joined Eisenhower for a game at Burning Tree at a time, Snead said, when the President "wasn't doing very well. [He] was losing sleep over the fact that his short backswing was causing him to lose power on his drives. The problem was so obvious I didn't hesitate to give him my advice: 'You've got to stick your butt out more, Mr. President.'

"His bodyguards couldn't believe I'd said that to the President of the United States. I couldn't believe it, either, but Ike was too intent on his game to notice.

"'I thought it was out,' he said."

The biggest limitation on Eisenhower's swing, however, was an eccentric left knee. He damaged it while playing football as a cadet at West Point, and it would pop out of place if he twisted that leg too sharply. The result was an exaggerated stiffness in his lower body as well as a restricted weight shift and hip turn during his downswing—all of which made him, according to one frequent partner, "a congenital slicer." At the same time, Eisenhower had unusually strong arms and wrists (when he was at West Point, he impressed others with the series of one-arm chin-ups he could perform), and that strength could on occasion produce an unexpected hook.

Yet when his swing was working, he was capable of cranking out drives in the 225-yard range. Sometimes, he could rip it even farther. Once, at the 10th hole at Augusta when he was playing with Nelson, Eisenhower nailed a drive that soared 260 yards,

When the Rains Came: Sam Snead held an umbrella for Ike, whom he saluted as "the greatest thing that ever happened to the game."
UPI/BETTMANN

surpassing Nelson's shot. "Both of them," reported Augusta's club professional Ed Dudley, "were surprised."

It was a moment Ike treasured. Like many a driving-range Hercules, he considered tee shots to be "the champagne of golf." But he had to fight a tendency to swing for glory. He could sometimes be heard muttering to himself on the tee, "Lord, just give me the strength to hit this thing easy."

The Top of His Game

Once Ike got close to the green, however, his approach shots were pure gold. "He plays his sand shots as well as almost any pro I ever saw," said Dudley, "and he's good with all of his short irons." Dudley cited particularly Ike's deft touch with his wedge and his 8- and 9-irons, which represented "the top of his game." In fact, one frequent partner practically supported his family on Ike's short game. That was James Hagerty, his press secretary, who had boundless confidence in his boss once his ball got within 80 yards of the flagstick—and backed up that faith with his wallet. "I don't know how much I've made on small side bets," Hagerty said, "figuring that when he's 70 or 80 yards away, he's going to get down in two. It seems that when I bet, he almost always does get down in two."

Hagerty pocketed five dollars one day at the Tamarisk Country Club in Palm Springs, California, thanks to perhaps the finest shot Eisenhower executed as President. His ball was stuck behind a palm tree 60 yards from the ninth green. Hagerty made his bet, and the President called for a wedge. His shot cut around the tree, landed on the green and stopped dead 18 inches from the pin. Eisenhower sank the putt, and Hagerty collected his five dollars.

Another Eisenhower strength was, as Hogan put it, "a good sense of course management. He's an accurate judge of the way a hole should be played, what club is required, how it should be used. He doesn't just pick up any old club, walk to the ball and hit it. I suppose such golfing attributes come natural in a General."

Hogan cited the way Eisenhower plotted his attack during their game on the third hole at Augusta, a 330-yard par 4. The

President drove the ball 220 yards against the wind and then faced a dicey second shot, with the pin at the back of a green that sloped away from him. After pondering the options, he punched a 3-wood off a bank to the right of the green; the shot kicked off the bank neatly on the first bounce and rolled to within 20 feet of the hole. "It was a shot well played and thoughtfully played," conceded the hard-to-please Hogan.

A *Major Weakness*

On the green, however, Eisenhower's short-game touch and sense of course management could desert him; he was, to put it kindly, an erratic putter. To overcome the problem, he experimented with all manner of cures—trying different grips, different putters, different pros—without much success. "If I could just make this thing work," he told one partner while staring glumly at his putter, "I'd enjoy the game a whole lot more."

The basic problem with Ike's putting, according to Clifford Roberts, was that he "was in too big a hurry. . . . He did not have the natural talent to read the greens correctly and he also did not seem to have sensitive fingers on his big-boned hands." But he might have overcome that if he hadn't been in such a rush. "He was too anxious to make the next shot," Roberts said. "He was always impatient to take a crack at the hole and, too often going far by, he would then miss coming back." Max Elbin, the veteran club professional at Burning Tree and former president of the Professional Golfers' Association, said, "I thought Gene Sarazen was a fast putter until I saw Ike. He acted as if he hated to putt and was anxious to get over to the next tee."

Elbin had a standard warning for those playing with Eisenhower for the first time. "I would tell them one thing," Elbin said. "'If you're riding with Ike, be sure and get into the cart quickly because he's not going to wait for you.' Hell, he'd hit his ball and you'd hit yours, and if you weren't back in the cart he'd damn near take off without you. Now, that's a little exaggerated. But he didn't fiddle around and wait for somebody."

The President rarely even took the time for a practice swing before his shots and, if he did, it was well away from the ball. "He don't pray over the ball," said Willie Frank "Cemetery" Perteet, who usually caddied for Eisenhower at Augusta National. "He just walks up to it, and off it goes."

Ike generally got off to a good start in a round. In fact, "he was one of the strongest starters I have ever seen," said club professional Norman Palmer of the Newport (Rhode Island) Country Club where the President played a number of times. He birdied the first hole there seven times in 22 rounds and rarely bogeyed it. "He played the hole like he owned it," Palmer added. "He also had a great facility for pacing himself during an 18-hole round. He finished pretty fresh most of the time."

During a round, said Hogan, "the President is companionable, good fun to play with. He has the trick of making you feel at ease. He convinces you, without saying so, that he likes the game as much as you do." A member at Augusta National put it more colorfully. Ike, he drawled, "is as natural as a Georgia watermelon."

Eisenhower enjoyed good golf jokes. One that he liked to tell involved two hackers who were standing over their shots a few yards away from the green. One lay eight, the other nine. The one who had taken nine strokes shrugged and said, "It's your hole. My short game is lousy."

Another favorite told of two golfers who were arguing about which one was worse. Finally, they decided to match scorecards.

"What did you have on the first hole?" asked one golfer.

"An X," said the other.

"Then you're one up."

But one thing about golf was no laughing matter to Eisenhower —and that was losing. He was a zealous competitor. There was the time, for instance, when the President was paired at Burning Tree with Bob Hope against General of the Army Omar Bradley and Senator Stuart Symington of Missouri. Hope didn't play well, so he and Eisenhower lost. The next day, they switched partners as the President and Bradley took on Hope and Senator Prescott Bush of Connecticut (a low handicapper and the father of President George

Bush). Hope, back on his game, shot a 75 and beat the President, with a press bet, out of four dollars. "I'll never forget the sour look on Ike's face when he pulled out his money clip and paid off," Hope recalled. "He looked me in the eye and grumbled, 'Why didn't you play this well yesterday?' He wasn't laughing, either."

When he was off his game, Eisenhower's neck would redden. Sometimes, after a bad shot, he would mutter ruefully, "Oh, boy. There's a typical Eisenhower." And occasionally, confided one partner, he would unleash some "five-star profanity—but softly." One memorable explosion occurred at the Eldorado Country Club in Palm Springs where a number of grapefruit trees bordered the fairways. During one round, the President's ball frequently strayed under those trees, and he was forever foraging among grapefruits on the ground to locate his ball. Finally, in exasperation, he roared, "When I get back to the White House, anyone who serves me grapefruit is fired!"

Birth of an Obsession

Ike didn't discover the delights of golf until age 37, when he attended the army's Fort Leavenworth (Kansas) Command School in 1927. He continued to pursue the game while stationed in Washington and the Philippines during the 1930s and even, occasionally, during World War II when he was the supreme allied commander in Europe. In the tense months leading up to D-Day, the Allied invasion of occupied France in June 1944, he would sometimes retreat to a suburban cottage outside London where he knocked balls around an adjoining golf course.

But it wasn't until Ike returned to Washington after the war as the army chief of staff that golf became an obsession. He began playing principally at Burning Tree and Augusta National. And he continued to golf just as avidly while serving as president of Columbia University in New York City and then as the supreme commander of the North Atlantic Treaty Organization in Paris.

Ike's infatuation with golf had been well advertised by the time he resigned the NATO command and ran for President as the Republican nominee in 1952. In fact, he managed to squeeze in a

Late Starter: Eisenhower, who didn't take up golf until age 37, is shown after a round in the Philippines during the 1930s. COURTESY, THE DWIGHT D. EISENHOWER LIBRARY

few rounds during the campaign and to shoot some quite respectable scores. He posted an 81 at Blind Brook, for example, and an 84 at his favorite course, the Cherry Hills Club outside Denver, Colorado. The electorate, thus, could have no excuse; they had been given ample warning that in Eisenhower they were getting a White House candidate who was the most devout golfer since Warren G. Harding more than 30 years before.

Only four days after taking the oath of office, Eisenhower was out on the White House lawn practicing his iron shots. A short time later, moreover, a golf group built a putting green, with a small sand trap to one side, for him just outside the Oval Office. Late in the afternoon, the President would typically grab some clubs and pad out of the Oval Office in his golf shoes.

Just outside the office, a small tee was set up in back of a clump of trees, and from there Eisenhower could lace out iron shots in the general direction of the White House fountain and

Ike at St. Andrews: As a five-star general in 1946, he hit his ball out of the rough while playing the historic Scottish course.

AP/WIDE WORLD PHOTOS

ornamental pool. His longtime orderly, Sergeant John Moaney, would be standing out there to retrieve the balls. Afterward, White House gardeners had to hustle around repairing divots in the lawn.

It wasn't long, however, before observant passers-by in the Ellipse noticed that one golf ball after another was raining down on the lower parts of the White House grounds. Soon, spectators and newsmen began gathering at the White House fence in late afternoons to watch the President practice. Some motorists even left their cars in the street in order to run over and take a look. So many did it that traffic jams began to develop.

It was an awkward situation. "I'm afraid I'm going to have to give up" the practicing, Eisenhower told a friend. "It's causing too much attention." Needless to say, he didn't stop. And by the spring, the problem solved itself. The leaves came out, shielding him from public view. When they fell in the autumn and people began watching again, he would duck into a police shack on the White House grounds and wait until they went away. He normally had to do that two or three times during each session. "You know," he said, "once in a while I get to the point, with everybody staring at me, where I want to go back indoors and pull down the curtain."

That was, in effect, an option. When the crowds or the weather drove him indoors, he would retreat to the small gymnasium on the ground floor of the West Wing of the White House where he had set up a special net. He would hit ball after ball into it.

The Attack of the Squirrels

The President had no problem with kibitzers on his putting green because it was hidden from public view. But he did have a problem with squirrels, who had been fed scraps by his predecessor, Harry Truman, and who kept burying acorns and walnuts in the green. Eisenhower was furious about this affront to golf and told Moaney, "The next time you see a squirrel go near my putting green, take a gun and shoot it!" The Secret Service, though, promptly stepped in to veto the command. "If there's shooting out there, we'd have to first inform the police," an agent explained. "So there'd be bound to be some fuss made, the press would get hold of it and the humane societies would never let you forget it. Couldn't some traps be set, instead?"

They certainly could, and the captured squirrels were trucked over to Rock Creek Park where they were set free. But squirrel-proofing the grounds proved to be more of a challenge than anyone had anticipated because an indignant conservationist kept releasing more squirrels through the White House fence until he, too, was finally apprehended.

Despite all his practicing, Eisenhower's game was not sharp during his first months in the White House. As a matter of fact, the job initially added eight strokes to his game, according to one fellow golfer, Governor Daniel Thornton of Colorado. One day, after the new President shot a 96 at Burning Tree, he announced grimly, "If I don't improve, I'm going to pass a law that no one can ask me my golf score." That prompted *Golf Digest* to issue thousands of round buttons with the words, "Don't Ask What I Shot."

A Big Secret

Indeed, for most of his presidency, Eisenhower's golf scores were kept a deeper secret than a movie actress's age. Many assumed that was because, if the scores were released, it would underline how much golf he was playing. But the real reason, it's said, was because Ike didn't want to put more pressure on himself. If he knew during each round that his score would be published in the press, he felt he would constantly strain to make good shots and, consequently, diminish his enjoyment of the game.

After his initial slump as President, Ike soon got his game working again—although his scores tended to relapse in times of crisis during his administration. He admitted that sometimes he found himself thinking about affairs of state "right in the middle of my backswing." Once, when he was agonizing about the plight of U.S. farmers, he growled that his "golf would be a lot better if somebody would do something about the price of beef."

"You can see it," said Hagerty. "He'll be going along playing really well—par, par, bogey, par, bogey. All of a sudden his mind comes off golf. Suddenly he's thinking about Quemoy or Lebanon or Berlin. Then it's triple bogey, double bogey and we all might as well go home. It isn't going to be any more fun that day."

Like William Howard Taft almost half a century earlier, Eisenhower caught a fair amount of heat because his pilgrimages to the links drew so much attention. According to one press survey early in his administration, "The President's golf game is on the front page of every paper daily." That may have been overstating the situation—but not by much.

Ike's play precipitated both criticism and derision. Senator Wayne Morse of Oregon, for example, lambasted the President for worrying more about his golf score than he did about the nation's unemployed. In their nationally syndicated newspaper column, Joseph and Stewart Alsop dismissed Eisenhower at one point as "a nice old gentleman in a golf cart." And at a press conference during a federal budget crisis, a reporter asked Eisenhower if he himself was prepared to economize by doing "without that pair of helicopters that have been proposed for getting you out to the golf course a little faster than you can make it by car." The President angrily denied the choppers were intended for that purpose.

At least one prominent critic confronted the President face-to-face. After a White House conference, labor leader Jacob Potofsky of the Amalgamated Clothing Workers of America interrupted an exchange of pleasantries to remark, "You know, Mr. President, we're keeping track of the number of times you play golf."

Presidential aides winced, but Eisenhower simply flashed his radiant smile. "You go right ahead," he replied. "I only wish that I could play more."

But Potofsky wasn't kidding. There really were those who kept a log of Ike's outings. Their records showed that, during his first year in office, he played golf 64 times—23 times in Washington and 41

An Impatient Patient: This editorial cartoon played off Eisenhower's yearning to get back to golf after his 1955 heart attack.
COPYRIGHT, 1955,
LOS ANGELES TIMES.
REPRINTED BY PERMISSION.

at vacation spots. The next year the total jumped to 85—27 times in Washington and 58 on vacation. So it went. By the end of his two terms, it's been calculated that he got in 800 rounds as President, or almost two per week.

Ike defended his frequent play by maintaining that golf got his "mind off everything else for a few hours. [And] there is the mild exercise, the kind that an older individual probably should have. . . . Now to my mind, that is a very useful thing, and I do it whenever I get a chance, as you well know."

The staunchest advocate of Eisenhower's golf was his physician, Major General Howard Snyder, who felt it was essential for the President to unwind on the golf course from the strains of his office. "If that fellow couldn't play golf," Snyder told a reporter, "I'd have a nut case on my hands."

The Allure of Augusta

Eisenhower first visited Augusta National in the spring of 1948 when he was looking for a place to unwind from his military duties. Clifford Roberts and New York publisher William Robinson had suggested the club might be the perfect spot—and it was. The Eisenhowers found the retreat in the rolling Georgia countryside completely to their liking, especially the privacy the club provided. Ike found the camaraderie and the golf especially appealing. According to Roberts, Ike's wife, Mamie, was taken with the place because she "liked the sound of a golf club better than a hunting camp or a fishing lodge."

Before long, Eisenhower decided to join the club, and the day after he won the presidential election of 1952 he flew to Augusta for a two-week holiday. The following year, his fellow members, a number of whom had served as unofficial advisers during his campaign, took up a subscription to build a cabin for the President about 100 yards from the clubhouse and the 10th tee. Actually, "cabin"—which is what the handful of such structures on the club property are called—was something of a misnomer since the building had two stories and could sleep eight people. Eisenhower

*Augusta's Big Three
(left to right):
Eisenhower with
Clifford Roberts and
Bobby Jones, the
co-founders of
Augusta National
and its Masters
tournament.*

AP/WIDE WORLD PHOTOS

accepted the cabin with the proviso that it be made available for
the use of other members.

Yet as much as he enjoyed his days at Augusta, Eisenhower
did have a nemesis there: the big loblolly pine tree that occupies a
spot in the left center of the fairway at the 17th hole. It acted
almost as a magnet for Ike's ball; no matter where he aimed

his drives, he invariably hit the tree. So when he sat in on one governors' meeting at the club, he proposed that the tree be cut down forthwith. "At this point," said then-chairman Roberts, "I decided that the only way to protect the club's property was to declare the meeting adjourned, which I did."

Decades later, it was still known as Ike's Tree.

Worst-dressed Club

Burning Tree was Eisenhower's preferred course when he was in Washington because it offered him a number of advantages: It was relatively nearby—10 miles from the White House, it was uncrowded since it had a limited membership, its perfectly groomed course was both fair and fun, its seclusion simplified the tasks of the Secret Service and it almost made a fetish of informality. There is a relatively loose dress code at Burning Tree, which once earned it a somewhat bittersweet designation as the "politest, worst-dressed club in the world."

Even the caddies joined in the laid-back spirit of the place. Not long after he'd become President, a couple of caddies watched Eisenhower tee off at the first hole at Burning Tree. His drive was badly off line, and one of the caddies snorted scornfully at it. The other caddie hissed, "Shut up—that's the President of the United States." Eisenhower teed up another ball, in accordance with a permissive mulligan rule at Burning Tree, and sliced that ball wildly.

"Mr. Lincoln," the first caddie exclaimed, "you sure liberated that one."

Ike's favorite caddie at Burning Tree became Allen "Napoleon" Whitehead. Before one round, Whitehead bet his caddie fee on the President, only to watch him break out in a rash of three-putt greens. Whitehead fumed as he saw his money melting away. Finally on the 16th green, Eisenhower stabbed at a 20-footer and sent it only halfway to the hole. Whitehead couldn't take it any more.

"For Christ's sake, Mr. President," he bellowed, "*hit* it!" Ike and his party laughed so hard, according to the Burning Tree club history, that no one could remember later whether he'd made his next putt.

Another caddie at Burning Tree was equally blunt during one round with Eisenhower, who on occasion would improve his ball's lie with his club, explaining that he was only trying to identify it. But during this particular round, he moved a ball too much, and it rolled a short distance against a rock. The caddie looked at Ike and said, "Mr. President, I think you overidentified that ball."

Generally, Eisenhower was as popular with his caddies as he was with the voters. His grandson, David Eisenhower, recalled that when caddies learned that Ike would probably be playing their course the next day, they would usually spend the night there, hoping to be first in line to be involved with the Eisenhower foursome.

Ike reciprocated by always including them in his on-course chatter. "We did all right on that shot," he might say. Or he might tease them after they handed him a club by saying, "If this isn't the right club, you'll be responsible." And he supplemented his customary five-dollar tip with two golf balls, each a high-compression model that was labeled "Mr. President."

The members at Burning Tree and Augusta National grew blasé about Ike's appearances at their courses. But it was a much bigger deal elsewhere. At the Newport Country Club, for example, club pro Norman Palmer said he got many requests from members asking if they could play with the President. They were all disappointed; the only players who shared rounds there with him were Palmer, two club officials and Francis Dwyer, the Republican congressman from Newport.

But the members were a crafty lot. When Eisenhower was in town, some would phone the club to determine his tee time the next day. They would then arrange to tee off before he did and be out on the course as he started to make his way around it. "They would deliberately play very slowly," said Palmer. "About the fifth tee, they would be waiting for us when we arrived." And they would always invite Ike's party to play through. "Of course," Palmer added, "they did this to get a close look and a spoken word from him."

Ike, however, did not particularly appreciate the favor. As a rule, he was reluctant to play through even the slowest foursome. So he would generally start his rounds early in the morning or afternoon in order to avoid catching up with other players. It seemed to put him off his game when he did. "Although holes were held open for him, he hated to play through other groups," recalled Burning Tree pro Elbin. "Once we were playing and the President was going great. Then we came to the 16th where another group was waiting. 'Oh, heck,' Mr. Eisenhower grumbled. Then his game just seemed to collapse."

A far graver problem developed in September 1955 after the President got in 27 holes one day at Cherry Hills while on vacation. That night he suffered a heart attack. It was the first of three illnesses that would strike in a three-year period. The next one, ileitis, occurred in June 1956, and the third, a mild stroke, hit him in November 1957. In all three cases, Eisenhower came back strongly to maintain his fervent golfing pace for the rest of his presidency—and into his retirement years.

The Ike and Arnie Show

After he left the White House, Eisenhower played most of his golf at Palm Springs and at Gettysburg, Pennsylvania, where he had a farm. And he could still have his days as a golfer. One of the finest came, when he was 73, at the historic Merion Golf Club course in Ardmore, Pennsylvania. There, he and that other great force in the postwar golf boom, Arnold Palmer, teamed up for a charity exhibition. Their opponents were professional Jimmy Demaret and entertainer Ray Bolger. Palmer would say later that "the General carried me"—and he wasn't just being politic. Eisenhower almost did; even his putter couldn't be denied that day.

Ike had never performed in front of a gallery before, and there were those who wondered how he would react. They needn't have worried. Off the first tee, he split the fairway with a 220-yarder, which brought a cry of "Hustler!" from Bolger. Playing an alternate shot format, Palmer then put Ike's ball on the green, and the former President stroked in a seven-foot putt for a birdie. There was no stopping him from then on. At the eighth hole, for instance, Palmer blasted a 320-yard drive into a downhill lie in the rough just in front of a yawning bunker. As he was addressing the ball, Ike turned to Palmer and said, "Arnie, forgive me for this." He then put the ball two feet from the hole.

"That man came to play," Palmer announced.

By the 16th hole, Eisenhower and Palmer had the match locked up three-and-two. Ike was running late for a dinner engagement at the nearby Valley Forge Military Academy, so an aide asked if he wanted to leave.

"The heck with it," Eisenhower replied. "Let's finish it." On the 17th, Palmer's tee shot hit the green, but fully 45 feet from the pin. Ike stepped up and rolled the ball over a series of undulations straight into the hole. The gallery roared, and *Golf* magazine reported that Eisenhower "beamed like a boy with a new bicycle."

But he saved the best almost for last. In 1968, the year before he died, the old soldier went out for a round at the Seven Lakes Country Club in Palm Springs with his favorite partner at the time, Freeman Gosden, the Amos of radio's long-running "Amos 'n' Andy" show. On the 104-yard 13th hole, a par 3, Ike launched a 9-iron shot that plopped on the green and proceeded to run straight into the cup—for his first and only hole-in-one. The 77-year-old Eisenhower put the achievement in a world-class golf fanatic's perspective. It was, he exulted, "the thrill of a lifetime!"

So much for all the rest of a storied career.

BOBBY JONES TO IKE: LIGHTEN UP

Dwight D. Eisenhower first met the peerless Bobby Jones in England during World War II, and they quickly became close friends. So close that after a neurological disease crippled Jones, he sent Eisenhower his personal set of clubs in 1951. They contained

Return Favor: Jones had given Eisenhower his personal golf clubs so Ike painted a portrait of Jones and presented it to the legendary champion. UPI/BETTMANN

the first steel-shafted driver to be used by a President as well as five woods, a set of irons, a sand wedge and a putter. Ike carried them in a red and black golf bag that had circlets of gold stars embossed on the side. Stuffed in one of the bag's pockets were golf balls engraved "Mr. President."

Eisenhower returned Jones's favor a few years later when he was President by painting an impressive oil portrait—actually it was a copy of one by the artist Thomas Stephens that depicted Jones during his golfing prime—and presenting it to him at the Augusta National Golf Club.

The two also corresponded frequently. Jones was always ready with some golf pointers. But he worried that the President's competitive nature was diminishing his enjoyment of the game. So on October 18, 1954, he sent the following letter to the White House:

Dear Mr. President:

I understand . . . that you have allowed some of your friends to more or less badger you into the idea of setting up competitions on the basis of your 18-hole medal score.

I want to suggest to you very seriously that this idea of playing for an 18-hole medal score can produce mental and nervous pressures to which you should not be subjected on the golf course.

A four-ball best-ball game giving you the opportunity to fail to finish a hole every now and then would be more relaxing and give you every bit of the atmosphere of competition which I know you desire.

If I were in your place, I would make up my mind that I would certainly never take a triple bogey and rarely a double bogey. I would just pick up the darn thing before that happens.

As ever,
Bob

CHAPTER 8

JOHN F. KENNEDY
A Closet Golfer

D uring his stretch drive for the presidential nomination in 1960, John F. Kennedy interrupted his strenuous campaign schedule in California to play golf with an old wartime buddy. On the par-3 15th hole at the Monterey Peninsula's exclusive Cypress Point Club course, Kennedy lofted a 7-iron shot that appeared to be heading for a hole-in-one. "I was yelling, 'Go in! Go in!'" recalled Paul B. Fay Jr., who was later to be undersecretary of the navy, while "Jack was standing there with a look of horror on his face."

The ball hit the pin and kicked to the side, about six inches from the cup.

With a sigh of relief, Kennedy turned to Fay and said, "You're yelling for that damn ball to go in the hole and I'm watching a promising political career coming to an end. If that ball had gone into that hole, in less than an hour the word would be out to the nation that another golfer was trying to get in the White House."

The panic inherent in those words was genuine; there were certain things that Kennedy preferred to keep hidden from the voting public. One, it later emerged, was his roving eye for women. Another, at this point in his career, was his love of golf. Indeed, according to Theodore Sorensen, one of his key White House aides,

A Stylish Swing: Kennedy struck the ball with a graceful, fluid motion that helped make him the best of all presidential golfers. UPI/BETTMANN

interest in the game as much as he could. Kennedy's scores were treated as state secrets, and he tried to avoid being photographed on the links. Indeed, he was apt to break off his game if press photographers were known to be in the area.

Publicity about Kennedy and his athletic family typically concerned such activities as touch football, a sport not likely to be viewed as elitist by voters. The strategy generally worked. When *Sports Illustrated* magazine ran a major article entitled "Sport on the New Frontier," for example, golf was given but a single, passing mention along with such other pastimes as swimming and skin-diving. As far as readers could tell from the article, the President's off-hours were spent mainly sailing. Not everybody was taken in by this, though. A few months after he was defeated by Kennedy for the presidency, Richard M. Nixon remarked that the only difference between Kennedy's golf and Eisenhower's was that Kennedy's was "a secret vice."

Kennedy went so far as to select courses that were out of the mainstream. Many of the golfing Presidents, for instance, were fixtures at the Burning Tree Club, the prestigious Bethesda, Maryland, layout popular with most Washington luminaries, including his predecessor, Eisenhower. Kennedy also was a member of Burning Tree at three different times—as a congressman; as a senator, when in an odd twist of fate Nixon was one of his sponsors; and as President (he dropped out twice during periods of ill health).

Kennedy did visit the Burning Tree course on many occasions during his White House years. But, according to golfing cronies, he often preferred to go to the Chevy Chase Club in suburban Maryland, which had a more narrow membership and where he was less likely to be spotted.

The President also liked to play at times when the fewest number of people would be on the course. On summer evenings, for instance, he would generally arrive at around six o'clock when the Chevy Chase fairways were likely to be relatively empty. He wouldn't begin at the first or 10th tee, either; after asking for a reading on which holes were open, he would start at the seventh,

Kennedy was deeply concerned that voters might find out about golfing "and kept those activities under cover during the campaig

This wasn't a matter of concealing the golfing pursuits of sc casual weekend duffer, a person capable of hitting an occasio lucky shot. Far from it. Kennedy was beyond question the b golfer ever to inhabit the White House. Despite a recurring b; ailment that plagued him for much of his adult life, he had a flu graceful swing, drove the ball impressive distances off the tee, p sessed a polished short game—and had the perfect attitude for gc He truly enjoyed the game. With all that going for him, he w capable of scoring consistently in the high 70s or low 80s.

Yet in the political wars of 1960, the candidate's affection f the sport was viewed as a severe handicap, something he and h advisers preferred to keep under wraps. Kennedy was, after all, Democrat, and his party, among other detractors, had tried to mak it look as if Republican Dwight D. Eisenhower had neglected th duties of his office because of his preoccupation with golf.

Kennedy was well aware of the criticism and worried about th impact similar charges might have on his candidacy. Moreover, h perceived golf as a hobby of the affluent, an aristocratic gam(played by young men who had inherited great amounts of money That, of course, aptly described Kennedy himself, but it certainl did not convey an image likely to curry favor with Democratic vot- ers. Kennedy feared being viewed in this light, according to one longtime golfing companion, because he believed that "the cham- pion of the common people shouldn't be playing a rich man's game."

State Secrets

After he was elected President, Kennedy delighted in showing vis- itors to the White House the marks that Eisenhower's spiked shoes had left in the floor of the Oval Office when he ambled outside to practice on the South Lawn. But he continued to conceal his own

The Right Stuff: Kennedy had the perfect attitude for golf. He truly enjoyed the game—and matches with family and friends in which he could needle his opponents. AP/WIDE WORLD PHOTOS

perhaps, and then move over to the eighth and finally switch over to the 15th and 16th—wherever play was the lightest.

After he entered the White House, of course, it was difficult for Kennedy to be inconspicuous. But even when he had Secret Service protection, he preferred minimum security. He would insist that he didn't want to arrive at a course with sirens blowing and lights flashing. And he asked that the Secret Service people stay out of sight as much as they could. Even so, playing companions were known to be more than a little disconcerted by the Secret Service men, who hid their weapons in golf bags; their presence had an understandable tendency to put an opponent off his game. (It could also be a little uncomfortable for the Secret Service people; on the only occasion when his press secretary, Pierre Salinger, persuaded the President to allow photographers a picture, at the first tee of the Palm Beach Country Club in Florida, his drive clipped an agent whose back was turned to him.)

All the Moves

Just about everyone who ever played with Kennedy commented on his relaxed, graceful swing. The President was athletic, had all the moves and looked like a golfer (he dressed in the khakis and colored tennis shirts popular during the period and was likely to show up in sneakers before changing into spikes in his cart). He had excellent tempo, good balance and knew what the game was about. Typically, he would tee off with a 3-wood but consistently hit his drives in the 220- to 230-yard range, usually with a slight right-to-left draw.

His prowess often surprised those who played with him for the first time. They'd say, "'Where in the hell did you get that good swing?'" related George Smathers, a onetime senator from Florida and frequent Kennedy golfing partner during the President's years in Congress and the White House. "You don't pick up that kind of a golf swing because you're now a senator or President and you acquire a beautiful swing. Hell no, that doesn't happen."

Actually, Kennedy's mastery of the game stemmed from his athleticism and an early start. He began playing when he was in his teens, unlike many other golfing Presidents who didn't take up the sport until they were fairly mature. His swing was a by-product of the aggressive world in which members of the Kennedy clan grew up; they were pressed to excel in a wide variety of sports. The Kennedy patriarch, Joseph P. Kennedy, a financier and onetime ambassador to Great Britain, was an enthusiastic if middling golfer, known for throwing clubs when he muffed shots and for being as fiercely competitive in low-stakes nassaus as he was when he was locked in $10,000 matches with his pals in Palm Beach.

The high point of the elder Kennedy's golf career had come in Britain during the first match he played there as the U.S.

Out of the Closet: JFK's love of the game was kept a deep secret until this photo appeared on the front page of The New York Times *in 1961. Golfing with Kennedy (left to right) were family members Stephen Smith, JFK's father and Peter Lawford.* AP/WIDE WORLD PHOTOS

ambassador. A hole-in-one he made on a course in Buckinghamshire was front-page news throughout Britain the next day, but Jack Kennedy and his brother Joe Jr. couldn't resist needling the old man by dispatching a telegram from home. "Dubious about the hole-in-one," it read. The feat, though, quickly became the subject of a quip the ambassador used regularly in after-dinner speeches. "I am much happier being the father of nine children and making a hole-in-one," he would say, "than I would be as the father of one making a hole-in-nine."

If he was intensely attentive as a father, he was somewhat less so as a husband. One year as the family was gathering to celebrate the birthday of his wife, Rose, the elder Kennedy realized he'd neglected to buy her a gift. All he could produce at the last minute was a box of golf balls, which was duly wrapped and presented.

Early on, Kennedy *père* urged young Jack to take lessons and played with him near the family's homes at both Hyannis Port, Massachusetts, and Palm Beach. So by the time he went to prep school at Choate, Jack Kennedy had already conquered the basics of the game. At Harvard, the future President competed briefly for the freshman golf team, earning his numeral on a squad that in the spring of 1937 amassed an undistinguished record of no wins, two losses and a tie. Kennedy participated in the match against Yale in the twosome and foursome competitions, losing in both events by lopsided scores of eight holes down with six to play.

Yet for much of his life, golf was a sometime activity for Kennedy, primarily because of an injury he suffered at Harvard. During his sophomore year in the autumn of 1937, he was an end on the junior varsity football team and one afternoon was dumped hard on a frozen field, sustaining damage to his spine that was to afflict him from then on. With his bad back, he never went out for the varsity golf team.

In later years, Kennedy was frequently hobbled by that back injury as well as other health problems—though most people were unaware of their true extent. The press featured articles on the fact that he used a rocking chair, under doctor's orders, to ease his aching back. But at times, usually out of public view, he limped around on crutches or was totally incapacitated. And he reinjured his spine on a number of occasions—once, for example, while sliding down a fire pole as a campaign stunt in Springfield, Massachusetts, and again during a tree-planting ceremony in Ottawa, Canada. There were times, too, when he had to be hospitalized; the most serious of them entailed a disk-fusion operation while he was a senator, which almost cost him his life. All told, his various physical problems kept him off the links for extended periods.

Still, Kennedy never lost his golfing touch, or his affection for the game. He hadn't played for five years when, during a campaign layover in the spring of 1960, he started swinging a club again and found it caused him no pain. A number of medical explanations were offered for the improvement. One was that the President began taking cortisone shots about this time, which helped make him look and feel healthier. Another credited a new exercise schedule that strengthened his back.

In any event, Kennedy surreptitiously took up the game once more—and the smooth swing he'd programmed as a youth was soon back in working order. One week after he'd won the election, he posted a 41 for nine holes at the Palm Beach Country Club—although his hands were still swollen and scratched from thousands of vote-seeking handshakes. Admittedly, the Palm Beach course was a comparatively easy one—it was not much more than 6,000 yards from the back tees. But Kennedy followed up with two separate 36s for nine holes and three times in a row birdied the tough ninth hole.

Truncated Rounds

During this period, Kennedy began playing a couple of dozen times a year, and while golfing partners found that he rarely complained about his back—except to direct a bit of profanity in its direction from time to time—he often played less than a full 18 holes. Smathers made this clear when he described the typical golf invitation from Kennedy as involving a call, saying, "'Old pal'—everything was 'old pal'—'what are you doing? Let's go out and hit a few. Let's go out and play a couple of holes.' It was never, 'Let's go out and have a round.'"

Consequently, it wasn't always easy to tell what scores Kennedy would actually have posted had he completed full rounds. He might birdie some holes, bogey some others, and on still others he might putt to six feet and say, "Hell, I'm not going to play it; give me a par." But his swing left no doubt about his talent.

Were invitations to golf with Kennedy anything like a command? "Not at all," said Congressman Jack Westland of Washington, who had been the U.S. Amateur champion in 1952. "It's the same as any other man being invited to play with the boss." He then added with a wide grin, "Of course, I can't think of any plans I might have that would be important enough to keep me from accepting."

At the time Kennedy was putting together his Cabinet, he played nine holes with Connecticut politician Abraham Ribicoff, who was rumored to be in line for a major post. When reporters subsequently quizzed Ribicoff about what had happened, he declined to say what job he had been offered but did comment that he had shot a 43 and that the President had beaten him by a stroke. Actually, Ribicoff had shot a 38 and Kennedy had a 42, and when the President read the press accounts, he had the following wire sent to Ribicoff:

> President deeply disturbed at newspaper report of your golf score, insists that anyone connected with his administration be clean as a hound's tooth. Write if you get work.

It was just a typical Kennedy prank, of course, and Ribicoff was soon appointed secretary of health, education and welfare.

What's the Soup?

Max Elbin, the professional at Burning Tree, contended that Kennedy could have scored even better had his mind not seemed to be on other matters. "If he had concentrated on it," Elbin said, "I think he could have shot in the middle 70s." Elbin observed that while other Presidents' schedules were arranged well ahead of time, "we never knew when Kennedy might pop in on us. He would drive up in a little car, step out and walk into the clubhouse. I recall once he walked right into the kitchen and asked the chef, 'What's the soup today?' The chef almost fell through the floor."

Kennedy played with short, whippy-shafted golf sticks, sometimes using Louise Suggs women's woods and irons. But whatever clubs he employed, and he often didn't even carry a full set, the strength of his game was his shorter irons. He could be erratic with his long irons, but his touch around the greens impressed his playing partners. Kennedy's 7-iron, the one he used for the near hole-in-one at Cypress Point, was probably his strongest club.

Companions reported that golfing with Kennedy was great fun in large measure because he didn't take the game too seriously. But

Kennedy on the Tee: The President played rapidly and didn't waste much time with practice swings. He'd simply tee up the ball, square his stance and let fly. AP/WIDE WORLD PHOTOS

it could also be unsettling since he liked to play very rapidly. In part, this was because of his habitual impatience, not to speak of an urge to get back to the affairs of state. According to Benjamin Bradlee, a Kennedy intimate and later executive editor of *The Washington Post,* the President's patience was so limited that on one particularly exasperating occasion, when Bradlee had hit a career drive that wandered only slightly off line, Kennedy flatly refused to stop and hunt for the ball.

This attitude also showed up in the way Kennedy approached his own shots. Typically, he did not take a practice swing. He'd simply address the ball, square up his stance and let fly. Nor did he waste much time lining up putts; how a putt was going to break wasn't of great concern to him. As a result, he was uncommonly generous in conceding putts to opponents: "Pick it up," he would say.

Presidential Gamesmanship

On the other hand, the President wasn't above gamesmanship. In fact, Press Secretary Salinger noted that "the smoothest part of his game was not the swing, but the 'con' he gave his opponents." Just before a companion was about to hit, Kennedy would sometimes point out sand traps, out-of-bounds markers and other hazards—"a courtesy," Salinger reported, "that would have taken the confidence out of a Ben Hogan."

He also had an edge available only to Presidents. On one occasion, Kennedy was at the Seminole Golf Club in Palm Beach with Chris Dunphy, an old friend and the club's chairman. At one hole, Kennedy hit an iron to within three feet and looked at Dunphy expecting the putt to be conceded. Dunphy looked away.

"This is a gimme, right?" Kennedy asked.

"Putt it," Dunphy responded. "That's the kind of putt that builds character."

"O.K.," Kennedy said, "but you disappoint me. Anyway, I had better hurry. I have a lunch date with the director of the Internal Revenue Service."

"That putt's good," he was told.

Similarly, the President once played with a senator from Indiana who was standing for reelection and whose state Kennedy was going to visit in support of the man's candidacy. When the politician holed a long putt in a match against him, the President called over to his aide, David Powers. "Dave," he said, "cancel that trip to Indiana."

On another occasion, when a scheduled outing was canceled by a heavy fog, Kennedy and Navy Undersecretary Fay went onto the White House lawn to hit balls. As Fay told the story in his memoir, *The Pleasure of His Company,* Kennedy selected Muggsy O'Leary, a security aide and golfing greenhorn, to chase the balls. "Muggsy," the President said, "of all the people who would have cherished this opportunity, you have been selected to be the first person to shag for the 35th President of the United States."

"What is shag?" responded O'Leary, in a tone that suggested he was not particularly impressed by the honor.

Kennedy told him to dump the balls on the lawn, then take the bag and go out so the players could hit iron shots at him. "From the expression on Muggsy's face," Fay noted, "I wasn't convinced that Muggsy didn't see himself as the first true martyr of the New Frontier." And when he turned around after walking only about 20 feet, the President confided, "Don't you get the impression that Muggsy hasn't quite grasped the true art of shagging?"

O'Leary moved out an appropriate distance, and Kennedy and Fay began to fire balls in his direction. The shots would rise into the air, quickly disappear in the fog and land somewhere perilously close to O'Leary. After a few minutes of this, Kennedy had a change of heart. "Muggsy," he shouted, "you're too valuable to this administration to risk you out there. Go back under cover." Finally, he and Fay took out wooden clubs and slugged balls over the Rose Garden, across the South Lawn and over the nearby trees. Fay reported that passers-by might have been startled to see golf balls emerging from the fog on the east side of the White House and bouncing down the street, but no one ever complained.

On the course, Kennedy could be as outspoken about the quirks of golfing fate as anyone. Bradlee noted that if he happened to shank a ball into the water, "he could let go with a broad-A 'bahstard,'" but he would instantly tee up another ball. On other occasions when he foozled a shot, Smathers recalled, "he would say things like, 'Jack, you dumb ass. Jeezus Christ, what kind of a dumb shot was that?' But he wouldn't cuss at anybody else; he would abuse himself. He would abuse the game."

Rub of the Green

Like his father, Kennedy usually had some bets going, although the stakes weren't as high. Bradlee described a 10-cents-a-hole match with the President and his sister-in-law Ethel in his book *Conversations with Kennedy*. At one point, Bradlee wrote, he asked Ethel what club she thought he should use, because he was unfamiliar with the course and a little unsure of his own judgment. She suggested a 5-iron. "I clocked it pretty good, only to see it go sailing way over the green," Bradlee noted. "I turned around to the sound of gales of laughter from Ethel and the President." It seems she wanted to win so badly, she intentionally suggested too much club—and the President found Bradlee's discomfort hugely amusing.

Kennedy often won many of his wagers before the first ball was hit because of a complex system of betting that only he fully understood. Salinger recalled that in addition to who won the hole there were bets on longest drive, first on the green, closest to the pin, first in the hole—plus automatic press bets when one team fell two holes behind and extra points for birdies and tee shots that hit the greens on par-3 holes. "No more than four or five dollars would change hands in a match," Salinger noted, "but JFK would play for it as if it were the national debt." General Chester Clinton, his military aide, learned this to his dismay one time when he was partnered with the President. The General left short a four-foot putt that would have halved the match, producing one of Kennedy's rare losses. "Nice putt, *Sergeant,*" Kennedy said.

Once in a while, the stakes in Kennedy's matches involved something other than money—such as, for instance, the cost of a dinner. In one case, Kennedy suggested to Smathers that they play for the price of a course in rapid reading, a subject that greatly interested him. "The course costs $125," he said, "and let's bet who pays for the other one's course." Smathers opposed the idea: "I said that's too much money. I can't afford it, and you have a rich daddy. So we bet a book, *The Advantages of Rapid Reading*. He won, and I had to buy him the book."

Passing the Buck

One reason Kennedy's betting often involved tangible items was the President's legendary reluctance to carry money. He grew up with more financial advantages than any other President, with the possible exception of Franklin D. Roosevelt. As Smathers put it: "He had all the money in the world. But the minute you'd be sitting somewhere and they would bring the check, he would start looking into [his shirt] pocket and say, 'Let me see if I've got any money.' When you see a guy looking into that pocket, you know you're in deep trouble." So after Smathers was exposed to three or four such incidents, he gave up. And henceforth, when the two men traveled together, Smathers would pick up all the checks, total up the bills, pay half himself and send the balance for payment to the Kennedy office in New York City. He didn't even bother talking to the President about expenses.

Among Kennedy's other frequent golfing partners were Dunphy, Fay, brother-in-law Stephen Smith, British Ambassador David Ormsby-Gore, brother Robert Kennedy, actor Peter Lawford and banker Charles Spalding. Once it was suggested that Kennedy play a match with Dwight Eisenhower to prove that he was a better golfer than his predecessor, but Salinger reported that the President rejected the idea as "frivolous."

On at least one occasion, Kennedy turned to golf to unleash his frustrations. That came early in his presidency right after the invasion at Cuba's Bay of Pigs, which he had authorized, proved to be a humiliating disaster. The next day, Spalding recalled, "We were just knocking golf balls aimlessly. And all he'd say is, 'How could I do it, how could I . . . ?'"

As a rule, however, Kennedy was something of a free spirit as he roamed the links and at times liked to conduct a running narrative. One of his favorite roles was that of TV golf commentator, and, as Bradlee related it, he would say things like, "With barely a glance at the packed gallery, he whips out a 4-iron and slaps it dead to the pin." When Kennedy was losing, Bradlee continued, "he would play the old warrior at the end of a brilliant career, asking only that his faithful caddie point him in the right direction, and let instinct take over. With his opponent comfortably home in two and facing a tough approach, he might say, 'No profile needed here, just courage,' a self-deprecating reference to his book *Profiles in Courage*."

Eventually, some reports of Kennedy's interest in the game began to appear in the press—and one person who spotted them was Cuban Premier Fidel Castro. Castro had repeatedly spoken of

Castro's Challenge: The Cuban leader, who called golf "a game of the idle rich," boasted he could beat Kennedy's score. He didn't come close.

AP/WIDE

WORLD PHOTOS

golf with scorn, terming it "a game of the idle rich and exploiters of the people." But he wanted to prove, he boasted, that "I could win easily over Kennedy."

So on a course across the bay from Havana, Castro set out over 18 holes with his revolutionary comrade Ernesto "Che" Guevara and another Cuban government official. Dressed in their olive-green army uniforms, wearing boots and the berets of the civilian militia, the Cubans teed off on the 6,692-yard, par-70 Colinas de Villareal course. Castro won the first hole. Guevara, who claimed to have once been a caddie in his native Argentina, won the second. But other than that, according to a contemporary press account, "there were no further details about the game."

However, an enterprising Associated Press reporter later cornered a 16-year-old caddie, who had helped carry the Cuban leaders' golf bags. He revealed that Guevara had shot 127 for the 18 holes and Castro himself had come in with a score in excess of 150. All of which went to prove that, despite the boasting, Fidel Castro was not a better golfer than Kennedy. But then, no American President has been, either.

Yet Kennedy continued to work on his game. And late in the summer of 1963, he commissioned White House photographer Cecil Stoughton to take some slow-motion movies of him as he played at Hyannis Port. The photographer filmed the President's putting and chipping strokes as well as his full swing—and kept his camera rolling after each shot, until the President indicated how well the ball had been hit and what direction it had taken. The method behind all this, Stoughton explained, was that Kennedy wanted "to be able to show an interested viewer how he approached the ball, struck it and the outcome."

The "interested viewer" Kennedy had in mind was Arnold Palmer. "I was to put these few weekends of film on a reel," Stoughton related, "and he was going to invite Arnie to the White House sometime later that year. He was anxious to get the critique from the master, but first he had to make a trip to Dallas in November."

JACKIE ON THE TEE

P resident Kennedy's wife, Jacqueline, on occasion followed him around in a golf cart, particularly when he was on holiday in New England. And she once gave her husband a birthday present of a "golf course" near their weekend retreat at the Glen Ora estate in Middleburg, Virginia.

Camelot on the Course: The President's wife, Jacqueline, got serious about the game for a while, took lessons and accompanied him on some rounds. But after his assassination, she never touched a club again. AP/WIDE WORLD PHOTOS

But when reporters got on to the story, White House press officials hastily pointed out that the "course" was actually a cow pasture, bearing little resemblance to a true golf course. Stakes had been set in the pasture to represent four holes. But the grass was so high, by one account, that each "hole" was assigned a par of nine, and the presence of cattle constituted a real hazard.

Jackie Kennedy, who later became Jacqueline Kennedy Onassis, got serious about the game herself for a brief period, taking lessons from professional Henry Lindner during several summers at the Newport Country Club in Rhode Island. "She went at it strong," Lindner recalled. "Never half way. And she liked to hit the ball hard."

A spokeswoman reported that after the President's death, his widow never played golf again.

The Perils of Riding with JFK

George Smathers, a senator from Florida and frequent Kennedy golfing companion, related an anecdote that revealed as much about Kennedy the man as it did about Kennedy the golfer. Kennedy, Smathers said, "was a terrible car driver and a terrible *cart* driver, but he wanted to drive all the time. He'd turn real quick and never tell you and damn near pitch you out of the cart. He was always that way."

The two men were riding in a cart one day at the Palm Beach Country Club in Florida when they came to a hole that had a walking path leading up to the green, surrounded on both sides by water. "If you took a cart," Smathers recalled, "you were supposed to go around the water. But this guy—he was forever doing something like this—tried to go where everybody walked. Across we went and all of a sudden over we went, the clubs and everything, into the water. Crazy. The biggest damn racket you ever heard. And he came out laughing.

"He said, 'Look at you. You're all wet. You went under. You went under.'

Scare Tactics: Kennedy flipped his golf cart, along with partner George Smathers (left), into the water at Palm Beach—an act, said Smathers, "typical of the Kennedy style and recklessness." AP/WIDE WORLD PHOTOS

"I said, 'Yeah. The damn cart was on top of me.' He got wet too; we were both in the water. But he laughed about it and went right on playing.

"This was the kind of thing that always tickled the hell out of him. He had a marvelous sense of humor, and he loved little things like that—anything that would get a big laugh where you looked a little stupid."

It was also, Smathers noted, "typical of the Kennedy style and recklessness."

CHAPTER 9

LYNDON B. JOHNSON
In the Land of the Eternal Mulligan

What hope of success in golf is there for a player of limited natural ability who isn't interested in playing a lot, in taking lessons or in spending any time on the practice range?

Ordinarily, the prospects would be grim. But if that golfer happens to be the President of the United States and has the brass of Lyndon B. Johnson, he can shoot some impressive rounds without the benefit of practice or frequent play. Of course, he needs to have something extra going for him—which Johnson did. It made him perhaps the slowest player of his time, but in the process it did guarantee a happy result on every hole.

Johnson's key to success in golf was simplicity itself. He never accepted a poor shot. If he hit a ball he didn't like, he would plop down another ball and hit again—and often again and again and again. As he made his way from tee to green, it could take as many as eight mulligans on each shot until he was satisfied. "He just hit until he liked one," said James R. Jones, the White House chief of staff during Johnson's last year in office. "He didn't say, 'Can I put down another?' He'd hit extra balls as if that were part of the game, as if that were the rule. He never let on that there was anything unusual about hitting all those balls."

Putting as Therapy: Johnson practiced his stroke on a green at the National Naval Medical Center in Bethesda, Maryland, following gall-bladder surgery in 1965.
UPI/BETTMANN

Nobody objected; he was the President of the United States, after all. And he did have an advantage over almost any other golfer in the world: He had a Secret Service detail on hand to chase down and collect all those unsatisfactory shots.

But LBJ did get teased about his mulligans. During one round on the course at an air force base in Puerto Rico, a crusty old sergeant was driving Johnson's cart. After several holes of multi-mulligans, the sergeant couldn't resist commenting that Johnson appeared to be heading for a very low score. "Mr. President," he said, "I think you're about to set a course record here."

Johnson brought to the game of golf none of the intensity and cunning that fueled his rise from the Texas hill country all the way to the White House, which he occupied from 1963 to 1969. "Golf," said White House aide Jones, "was not something Johnson set out to conquer." That was mostly because he lacked two indispensable qualities as a golfer. First, he wasn't much of an athlete. As Bob Hope said after playing with him once in Acapulco, "He didn't seem to have much touch or feel for the game." Second, LBJ was always too preoccupied with politics to concentrate enough to compensate for his deficiencies on the course.

Why He Didn't Suffer

He was, however, a most amiable golfing companion. The President, said Burning Tree pro Max Elbin, "didn't play very well, but he had a hell of a good time. He would josh around, kidding whoever was with him. He'd make comments to the other players—of a personal nature." His score was of little concern to him (which was fortunate because there's no record that he ever broke 100 while counting only first strokes). He was out there for fun or politicking or both, and he moved along blithely taking all those mulligans and laughing most of the way. He played "with an abandon that was most literally carefree," a Burning Tree club history reported. "He was the only President—and perhaps the only golfer—who never suffered on the course."

For appearance's sake, Johnson tried to be secretive about his golf just as his predecessor, John F. Kennedy, had been. LBJ's visits to Burning Tree were not listed on his official daily schedules, and he traveled to and from the club in an unmarked car. "He always had the theory," Jones reported, "that the more you show force and the more you advertise security, the more the nuts will be determined to get through it and try to knock you off." And he tried to be as inconspicuous as possible on a golf course. Once, when he thought he might be spotted by some photographers, he immediately turned around and sought the clubhouse for cover.

Inevitably, of course, word did leak out about his golf and his many shortcomings as a player. James Reston commented in his column in *The New York Times* that "lately the President has shown a vague interest in golf. . . . Golf is a plague invented by the Calvinist Scots as a punishment for man's sins, and nobody has yet found anybody in Washington the President can beat."

Johnson had once remarked that "one lesson you'd better learn if you want to be in politics is that you never go out on a golf course and beat the President." Now, though, he had to concede that the advice made no sense, at least in his own case. After he was told of Reston's column, he said kiddingly that he had been slandered. But

The Multimulligan Man: During this round in Puerto Rico, Johnson took so many mulligans before accepting good shots that his cart driver remarked he was headed for a course record. AP/WIDE WORLD PHOTOS

he then added, "I guess it's possible to slander a person and still tell the truth. What he [Reston] said is true."

A Problem Swing

LBJ never took a lesson—and it showed. He held his club using a baseball grip, and he swung for the seats. One observer said, "He went at the ball as though he were killing a snake."

Johnson took an upright stance as he addressed the ball with his legs fairly stiff. He was a big man, standing 6 feet 3 inches tall and weighing between 230 and 240 pounds. So he had a big belly to swing around, and that hampered his form. His swing, in fact, was all arms with little body turn. Elbin of Burning Tree said that "he was a fellow who slammed down with his hands and arms and took a hell of a lot of turf. He was a digger. He'd move his hands too early from the top of the backswing, and that would mean knocking off a big chunk of turf and not getting much out of the ball."

When he really connected with a drive, though, his heftiness could help send the ball a prodigious distance. "He was wild as hell," Chief of Staff Jones recalled. "He might hit the ball 300 yards, or it might dribble two feet in front of him." The same inconsistency afflicted his short game. But his putting wasn't bad, according to Jones.

All that explained Johnson's response when a reporter asked him what his handicap was. The President replied jovially, and quite correctly, "I don't have a handicap. I'm all handicap."

Golf was never among Johnson's higher priorities—although a golf course seemed to be one of the few places where he could truly relax. Otherwise, said Jones, "he was a politician 24 hours a day. Everything he did had a purpose to it . . . and it was usually politics of some sort." He regarded those who took time regularly for recreation as plain and simple sluggards.

"He did understand dimly that other people had some interests outside of their direct work," wrote George Reedy, the President's press secretary. "But he thought of such interests as weaknesses. I cringed every time he attended a baseball game because he made it

Golfing with Eisenhower: Johnson sought the old soldier's advice on the Vietnam War but upset Ike by winning his only hole when the press was watching. UPI/BETTMANN NEWSPHOTOS

so perfectly obvious that he was bored by the whole procedure. He went only when a game was to be attended by a large number of fellow politicians with whom he could transact some business. On such days, I sat at home praying that television cameras would not catch him with his back turned to the field in deep conversation about a tax bill or an upcoming election while a triple play was in progress or when a cleanup hitter had just knocked a home run with the bases loaded."

Johnson sometimes used golf with much the same kind of purpose in mind—although he always had fun doing it. The most notable such occasion came in February 1968 when he visited Dwight D. Eisenhower to seek the old soldier's advice on the conduct of the Vietnam War, which was then generating a storm of domestic protest. The two met at Eisenhower's retirement home in Palm Springs, California. As they set off to play a round at the Seven Lakes Country Club, Ike was looking ruddy and red, and he was wearing a bright yellow golf shirt. That contrasted with LBJ's relatively pale complexion and austere gray garb. Jones accompanied them on the round (in which there were no mulligans asked or given), and he described it this way:

"Eisenhower took his golf quite seriously, and Johnson would hit the ball all over the place. And Eisenhower was just steady, right down the middle—150 yards or whatever. There was no money on it. They just talked and played. And Eisenhower won, as I recall, every hole until the 18th. It was a dogleg right. While the press was all kept away from photographing [earlier holes], they were all at the 18th hole.

"Johnson teed off on the 18th right down the middle. I don't know how long, but it was a long hit. Then he was on in two and parred. Eisenhower lost the hole with just another steady bogey, and Johnson won. Eisenhower was not a particularly gracious loser of the hole—even though he won the match—because the hole Johnson won came in front of the press. Eisenhower had a certain edge to his voice, like you were dogging it all this time but when the chips were down. . . . It was the pride of performing in front of the press."

Playing without the aid of mulligans, Johnson finished with a score "a little over 100," according to Jones.

LBJ had less success in a match with British Prime Minister Harold Wilson. "I shot a 76, and the President was in triple figures, so a discussion followed," Wilson said afterward with a straight face. He then added with a sly smile, "We were trying to decide whether to play the final nine holes."

Johnson put golf to nonpolitical purposes, too. In the middle of his term, for example, the White House invited Arnold Palmer to drop by with a set of his signature clubs to present to visiting General Ne Win, the Burmese strongman who was an avid 10-handicap golfer. Through some snafu, the General got a set of Wilson clubs. But Palmer's clubs didn't go to waste. A few days later, President Ferdinand Marcos of the Philippines showed up, and he received the Palmer set.

Johnson got some golf goodies himself. He once admired a pair of soft yellow pigskin golf shoes worn by the Reverend Billy

Graham. The next time Graham visited the New York store where he'd acquired the shoes, he said, "I bought a pair of them in Mr. Johnson's size in every available color—six, I think—and sent them to him."

His Sports Experience

The President had almost no background in sports to call upon when he took up golf. There had been little time or money for games during his youth. (When West German Chancellor Ludwig Erhard met LBJ for the first time, he said, "I understand you were born in a log cabin, Mr. President." Johnson replied, "No, Mr. Chancellor, I was born in a manger.") Johnson did play some baseball as a youth—although it was on his terms. He was one of the few kids in the poor Texas hill country town of Johnson City who could afford a baseball. According to LBJ biographer Robert Caro, Johnson "insisted on pitching although he was a terrible pitcher. And he would do literally what we kid about. He would take his ball and go home if he couldn't pitch."

But almost from the beginning, Johnson had one all-consuming interest: politics. When he watched baseball games as a young man, for instance, he would argue politics through every inning. Said one friend, "Sports, entertainment, movies—he couldn't have cared less. [His focus] was so narrow it was almost ludicrous."

LBJ lightened up—a bit, anyway—after he arrived in Washington as a congressman in 1937 and decided to play a little golf. It was good exercise and a relaxing diversion from his workaholic schedule. Beyond that, according to his wife, Lady Bird, "he especially liked to take advantage of the time he spent on the course to explain ideas and for discussions in a relaxed setting." (Although Lady Bird never golfed, the municipal golf course in Fredericksburg, Texas, near the site of the Johnson ranch, is named after her.)

Johnson's occasional partner during his early years in Washington was Eugene Worley, a young fellow congressman from Texas. (This was in LBJ's premulligan days.) Worley recalled that the first time they played, at the Army-Navy Country Club in Arlington,

Virginia, Johnson complained that his game was rusty. "All that he was doing," Worley said, "was leading me up to spot him a stroke a hole.

"We didn't have much money. We were playing, I think, for a quarter—a quarter nassau. So he talked me into the stroke a hole, and sure enough we finish the 17th hole and I'm 50 cents down.

"I said, 'Lyndon, I ought to play you double or nothing on the 18th [a par 4] and still give you a stroke on the hole.' I was trying to get my money back.

"He said, 'Aw, no.'

"I said, 'Well, why not? What can you lose? You're playing with my money.'

"He said, 'Hell, I didn't work 17 holes just to give it all back to you on one hole.' And he didn't."

Sizing Him Up

Even so, Worley liked Johnson's style. "There are three ways you can sort of size up a fellow," Worley observed. "One's playing golf with him, one's drinking with him, and one's playing poker with him. Well, I did all three with [Johnson], and he measured up to every standard that I would ask for in a man. You never caught him cheating. He'd try to bluff the devil out of you; he was like Harry Truman in that respect. But he generally had something to back it up."

Years later, when he was the Senate majority leader, Johnson temporarily gave up golf following a heart attack in 1955. But he'd resumed the game by the time of the 1960 presidential campaign when he was elected Vice President on the Democratic ticket headed by Kennedy. In fact, one of the first things Kennedy and Johnson did after winning the election was to play a clandestine round of golf together in Palm Beach, Florida.

During that campaign, Johnson had been of two minds about all the golf played by Eisenhower, the then-incumbent Republican in the White House. In June, LBJ said, "I'm glad he does [play golf]. I want him to have all the rest that he can get." That attitude differed sharply from the Democratic party line that derided Ike for his constant rounds of golf. By October, Johnson had adopted the party line. During a whistle-stop trip through the South, he charged that "for eight long years the South has been used [by Republicans] only as a golf course to tee off from," a reference to Ike's frequent excursions to the Augusta National Golf Club in Georgia.

Their criticism of Eisenhower's golf, of course, forced Kennedy and Johnson to keep their own play under wraps when they each in turn became President. Johnson even insisted initially that high officials in his government keep a low golf profile. When he ordered Secretary of Commerce John Connor off Washington area courses on weekends, he explained he didn't want an "Ike golf image" for his administration.

Johnson had an added reason for the early furtiveness about his own golf. He was fearful of what it would look like if he was portrayed as playing golf while U.S. troops were fighting and dying in Vietnam. One evening, when he was feeling particularly imprisoned in the White House, he had a beer with an aide and lamented, "The Temperance Union would be on my ass [if they knew about the beer], I can't play golf because they'll think I'm frivolous, I can't do this, I can't do that. . . ."

Johnson also had to be extra careful about his public appearances for fear he might spark embarrassing antiwar protests. But one Sunday, his aides weren't careful enough. The President was scheduled to attend church that morning before sneaking off for a round of golf. He asked White House Chief of Staff Jones ahead of time whether the church's minister had been checked out for his views on Vietnam. Jones asked a Secret Service agent who assured him that the minister was "very reputable." But during the church service, the minister proceeded to preach a sermon that sharply criticized Johnson's policies in Vietnam. The President was furious. When they played their round of golf after church, Jones said, Johnson "chewed on my ass for 18 holes. The whole time. It was the worst golf I ever played."

Gradually, the President got less sensitive about golfing in public. Late in his term, he played that match with Eisenhower and on occasion he even used the putting green outside the Oval Office that had rarely been played on since Ike left the White House. But LBJ didn't putt with much success. Once, as the press looked on, he failed to sink three putts each from six and eight feet. And shortly before he declared that he would not seek reelection as President in 1968, he had relaxed enough about the game to take a one-day golf vacation in Puerto Rico. It was the first announced holiday the President had taken after four and a half years in office. A major newspaper was so astonished by this development that it headlined its article about it: "Johnson Takes a Whole Day Off."

Golf versus Whiskey

Indeed, the President got so comfortable about golf that he remarked in jest that he was giving up whiskey and taking up golf instead. Reston of *The New York Times* responded in kind in his column:

> The United States has had Presidents who drank but did not play golf [Jackson and the second Roosevelt while in office]. It has had Presidents who did both [Taft and Eisenhower]. But diligent research turns up nobody before Johnson who tried to escape from his worries by giving up liquor and taking up golf at the same time. . . . To substitute golf for "whiskey's old prophetic aid" is a puzzle and could be a calamity. And to do it as an escape from agony is the worst miscalculation since the start of the Vietnam war. Golf is not an escape from agony. It is itself an agony.

Actually, Johnson at the time was thinking more about the years ahead after he left the White House. He told Elbin of Burning Tree, "I just want to [play well enough] so that when I get out of this job

I can use golf as a winter sport." He did golf occasionally during his retirement in Texas, but it never really became his "winter sport."

"In a very important sense," wrote Press Secretary Reedy, "LBJ was a man who had been deprived of the normal joys of life. He knew how to struggle; he knew how to outfox political opponents; he knew how to make money; he knew how to swagger. But he did not know how to live."

BARRY GOLDWATER: ONE OF THE BEST

Senator Barry Goldwater of Arizona, the conservative Republican who Lyndon Johnson beat in the 1964 national election, was certainly one of the best two or three golfers ever to win the presidential nomination of any political party. Goldwater grew up in a golfing atmosphere, and no less an authority than Sam Snead called

Presidential Candidate Goldwater: He impressed Sam Snead when they won a Phoenix Open pro-am event.

AP/WIDE WORLD PHOTOS

him a "good golfer" who could be a "fine one if he wanted to concentrate on the game. But he's too busy. His game suffers from lack
of practice. You can see it. . . . I figure he could be a five-handicap
man."

Snead based this assessment in part on Goldwater's performance
when they played together one year in the Phoenix Open pro-am
and won the event. The tournament went well for the two of them
except for one hole where the senator drilled a tee shot that struck a
spectator standing some 30 yards away. Goldwater apologized, of
course, but later explained the incident with this quip: "The guy
was standing too close to my ball."

Goldwater's most quoted golf remark stemmed from the fact
that his father was Jewish while his mother was an Episcopalian and
he was raised in that faith. (The remark has also been attributed by
some to Goldwater's brother, Bob, a scratch player who at one point
held the Arizona state championship.)

It seems that Goldwater showed up to play at a country club in
Arizona where a sign was posted outside the clubhouse that read,
"Gentiles Only." When Goldwater walked onto the practice area to
warm up, the club manager came running out and pointed to the
sign.

"Mr. Goldwater," he said, "I'm afraid you won't be able to play
here because of our rules."

"That's all right," Goldwater replied. "My mother was an
Episcopalian, so I'll only play nine holes."

CHAPTER 10

RICHARD M. NIXON

You Don't Have to Be Good to Play Well

By all accounts, Richard M. Nixon was not among the most athletic of Presidents. His first chief of staff in the White House, H. R. Haldeman, once described him as the least dexterous man he had ever known. "Clumsy," Haldeman noted, "would be too elegant a word to describe his mechanical aptitude." And when it came to golf, Nixon brought to the links a swing that could charitably be described as awkward, flat-footed and jerky. The President's technique, one sportswriter observed, made him look as if he were beating a carpet that hung behind him.

Yet if Nixon wasn't a graceful golfer, he more than made up for it with two other qualities that can lead to success on the links: determination and perseverance. He wanted to play well and was willing to work countless hours to that end. Indeed, because of his tenacity, said teaching professional Max Elbin of the Burning Tree Club, Nixon "improved as rapidly as anybody I ever saw."

Nixon came late to the game; he did not begin to play until he was 37 years old. But once he got serious about golf, he quickly got to the point where he could score fairly consistently in the low 90s or high 80s. He reported that within six years of the time he first picked up a club, "I surprised everyone, including myself, by becoming a 12-handicap at Burning Tree."

Practice Makes Perfect: Nixon wasn't much of an athlete, but long hours of practice on the range produced a workmanlike game—and this grin after a hole-in-one at Bel-Air Country Club in Los Angeles. UPI/BETTMANN

Like most of the golfing Presidents, Nixon found that the game provided him with much-needed relief from the pressures of the job. He believed that getting away from the Oval Office was "absolutely indispensable" for the man who holds the toughest job in the world. But later, after he had resigned the presidency in disgrace in the wake of the Watergate scandal, the game played an even more important role for him.

"Golf became my lifesaver," he declared.

It was then that Nixon found consolation in the special rewards of the game—not only exercise and competition but what he described as "warm companionship." Nixon was a man generally portrayed as something of a loner, especially when sports were involved. Newspapers of the day, for example, carried photographs showing the President as a solitary bowler, primly dressed in a tie and shirt as he hurled the ball down the alley in the White House. But Nixon could loosen up in a golfing environment, as he proved one day in California at Hollywood's Lakeside Golf Club.

After a round with show-business celebrities Bob Hope, Fred MacMurray and James Stewart, Nixon was chatting in the Lakeside locker room with comedian George Gobel. According to the club's history, Gobel said he had to get home but cracked, "I didn't think it was polite to undress in front of a President." Replied Nixon, with a shrug, "Well, it's your locker room, George." Gobel then announced he would call his wife, Alice, but expressed concern that she'd never believe he was late because he was having a drink with the President of the United States.

Nixon offered to speak to Alice Gobel and, while everyone in the locker room held his breath in fear of how she might respond, the conversation went amiably. Nixon explained why the comedian was late and, with a wink—"It was the first time I've ever been winked at by a President," Gobel said—promised to send her the monogrammed ball he had used that day.

As the men were about to leave the locker room, Gobel quipped, "Gee, I wish he hadn't told Alice about the ball, because I was going to give it to a broad in New York."

When Nixon heard the remark, he tapped Gobel on the shoulder and whispered, "Don't worry, George, here's another golf ball for that broad in New York."

Beyond the camaraderie, Nixon discovered that golf had an appeal that nonplayers never get to enjoy. He noted that golf courses are located on the most beautiful real estate in the world—an attraction once pointed out to him by Senator George Smathers of Florida. "I hadn't thought about it in that way, but he was right,"

the President observed, citing the kick he got out of playing such
"spectacular" courses as the Cypress Point Club in Pebble Beach,
California; Augusta National in Georgia; Oak Hill Country Club
in Rochester, New York; Baltusrol Golf Club in Springfield, New
Jersey; and Bel-Air Country Club in Los Angeles. Of them all, he
said, his favorite was the 6,248-yard Valley Club course, a lesser-
known layout in Santa Barbara, California, designed by noted architect Alister Mackenzie, who also fashioned Augusta, Cypress Point
and such other world-renowned courses as the Royal Melbourne in
Australia.

Pointed Hint

Nixon's real introduction to the game came from that most fanatical of White House golfers, Dwight D. Eisenhower. During
Nixon's terms as his Vice President, Ike tried to make a sportsman
out of him. First they tried fishing and the fine art of casting for
trout. It was, as Nixon related it, "a disaster. After hooking a limb
the first three tries, I caught his shirt on my fourth try. The lesson
ended abruptly."

A few months later, Ike invited Nixon to give it another shot—
this time at golf. Here Nixon had a little more experience, though
he was barely beyond the beginner stage and sported a high
handicap. One day in the spring of 1953, Eisenhower asked his Vice
President to be his partner in a match at Burning Tree. Ike figured
that Nixon had to be better than his handicap indicated and should
be able to help the team. But when the duo lost the match—and
the bet—Ike was not amused. As Nixon described the event in his
memoirs, "He talked to me like a Dutch uncle. 'Look here,' he
said. 'You're young, you're strong and you can do a lot better.'"

In a very real sense, then, Eisenhower shamed his Vice President
into approaching the sport more seriously. Nixon began to take
lessons, to practice and to play more often. And while he came
to enjoy the game for its recreational value, intimates claim he
was also inspired by a desire to beat Eisenhower. He reportedly
did so once as Vice President, shooting an 84—much to Ike's

*Following the Leader:
Dwight D. Eisenhower
shamed his Vice
President into taking
golf seriously by scolding
Nixon about his failings
on the course.*

UPI/BETTMANN

consternation. But when asked about it years later, Nixon responded diplomatically that "the reports that I beat Eisenhower are inaccurate. Whenever I played with him we were partners, as we were in political campaigns."

The determination that Nixon showed in learning golf reflected a trait that was very much part of his personality. It first showed up in sports during his school days when he was a bench-warming, 150-pound lineman on the football team at Whittier College in California. Teammates wondered why he continued to go out for the team since he was routinely knocked about and bloodied in practice scrimmages ("cannon fodder," one of his friends called him) and rarely got into games.

But Nixon was a shrewd analyst of play, gave pep talks at halftimes and, on those occasions when he was allowed on the field for a few minutes, drew cheers from the Whittier crowd. He frequently jumped offside in his eagerness, but he profited from the whole experience. "Being a loser begins to help after a time," Nixon once observed, noting that it's natural for Americans to root for the underdog.

He also contended that he learned more from his football coach, Wallace "Chief" Newman, than from just about anyone he had ever known. Newman was an early-day, winning-is-the-only-thing version of Vince Lombardi, and Nixon credited Newman with teaching him that, even when you're defeated, "you don't quit. When you lose, you fight harder the next time." That clearly left its mark on Nixon the politician; eight years after losing the presidential election of 1960, he came back to win the White House. It also prepared him for the ordeal he was to undergo when he took up golf.

On the Lesson Tee

Nixon was nearly 40 years old when he brought his game to Elbin at Burning Tree. As a senator, he had taken one informal lesson from golfing legend Sam Snead, who advised him to chip with a wedge. But now he said to Elbin, "I don't want any of that top-drawer stuff. I just want to know how to play the game." In other words, as the pro translated it, he didn't want a lot of confusing theories; he simply wanted to learn the basics and take it from there.

Nixon grasped the club with a baseball grip, which Elbin promptly changed to the standard overlapping grip. And Nixon's inexperience was underscored by the way he squatted to put his tee in the ground. But after learning some fundamentals about swinging the hands, then the arms and making a shoulder turn, he immediately wanted to play. As Elbin described the result, when the two men teed off, the Vice President hit his first shot into the parking lot.

Elbin gave Nixon three or four more formal lessons on the practice tee, as did teacher and club designer Toney Penna, who also presented him with a set of his clubs. The Vice President became "a keen student of the game," Penna reported, and his scores began to improve. Before long Nixon was playing regularly at Burning Tree, but he still had a lot to learn. Harold Bell, a sports talk show host who caddied for the Vice President in those days, recalled that he referred to his Burning Tree rounds as "an adventure." Bell said that at first he didn't fully understand the remark, but "after three holes," he did—Nixon's "golf balls spent more time in the trees than most squirrels."

Nixon's most frequent golfing partner at Burning Tree was William Rogers, the attorney general in the Eisenhower administration and, when Nixon became President, his secretary of state. And during one of their early outings, Nixon made a crucial breakthrough.

It seems Nixon and Rogers played the first hole at a leisurely pace and were overtaken on the second tee by a faster-moving foursome, which included Eisenhower. Following the club's protocol, Nixon invited Ike's group to play through and moved out of the way. Eisenhower and two members of his group reached the fairway with their drives, but the fourth player heeled his ball into the woods to the left of the tee. The foursome plunged into the underbrush to look for the ball, and moments later Ike called back to Nixon to go ahead. Nixon declined. The President insisted. But Nixon still declined.

At last, Ike's luckless partner found his ball and managed to get it back into play, and the Eisenhower foursome moved ahead. But the incident was particularly significant because it made Nixon aware that golfing embarrassments are commonplace—and after that, club documents related, his game "steadied."

Gradually, Nixon began to develop two strengths to his game. He could drive the ball straight and fairly well, usually in the 175-to-200-yard range. As he put it, "My wood shots were accurate but not long." He also displayed a good putting touch. When he got to the green, he had confidence that he could knock the putt in. If a person can drive and putt, Elbin observed, "I don't care who he is. He can score as a general rule." And that's what happened with Nixon. His scores continued to improve, until one day, while playing with Elbin and touring pro Jimmy Demaret, he posted an 87. "It was legitimate," Elbin declared.

Eventually, according to Nixon, the best part of his game was from 100 yards in. His favorite club was a MacGregor 11-iron, which he said he learned to use with great accuracy: "The late Johnny Reardon, the pro at Spring Lake Country Club in New Jersey, taught me how to use it by making me practice for hours pitching over traps."

Nixon also became more involved in casual play at Burning Tree, participating in the Sunday Foursomes event on several occasions. Pat Buchanan, later a journalist and a presidential candidate himself, recalled caddieing for the Vice President at Burning Tree in those days and carrying his distinctive plaid golf bag. Buchanan reported that even as a 15-year-old caddie he could see that Nixon's swing was awkward, "yet from the comments his fellow players made, you'd have thought we had the young Palmer out there. 'Great shot, Dick, a real beauty,' one said . . . as the Vice President popped a 150-yard drive down the fairway."

Once Nixon even entered the club championship at Burning Tree, qualifying in a middle-range flight. There, he lost to political writer William Lawrence of *The New York Times*—but only on the 18th hole, and only after Lawrence parred it. Finally, for a brief time in 1958, Nixon could claim a 12-handicap. But the next year, he gave up the game temporarily to prepare for his run for the presidency against John F. Kennedy—whom, ironically, he had sponsored for membership at Burning Tree some time earlier.

What Hole-in-One?

After he narrowly lost the 1960 election to Kennedy, Nixon had more time on his hands, and he resumed playing golf. The next year he achieved the million-to-one shot, making a hole-in-one. "I don't remember much about it," he noted, downplaying the event in his memoirs. Yet he then went on to recall, "It was on the third hole at Bel-Air on Labor Day, 1961. I used a MacGregor 6-iron and a

Going Hollywood: Nixon's dour personality became more playful when he relaxed with celebrities such as (left to right) James Stewart, Fred MacMurray and Bob Hope, here at the Lakeside Golf Club. AP/WIDE WORLD PHOTOS

Spalding Dot ball, and my partner, [actor] Randolph Scott, birdied the hole." His ability to remember those details suggests that Nixon must have been somewhat more excited about the event than he let on; indeed, he had his scorecard framed and later called the experience "the biggest thrill I had playing golf." Yet when Eisenhower wrote to congratulate him, saying that he [Eisenhower] was taking all the credit, Nixon admitted in his response that, despite the hole-in-one, he had shot a 91 and wound up losing three dollars.

Nixon moved East after an unsuccessful bid in 1962 for the governorship of California and from 1965 to 1968 was a member of Baltusrol and frequently played there with some of his New York law partners. On the demanding Baltusrol course, which has hosted numerous U.S. Open championships, he had a respectable handicap of about 16. Nixon resigned, according to the Baltusrol club history, after the press attempted to make his membership in the exclusive club "a political issue." What happened was that when reporters questioned his membership in a restricted club, Nixon responded, "I'll try to change the club's policy from within" (he resigned four months later). Yet subsequently, when one of his federal appointees was criticized for having held a similar membership, Nixon said that if everybody who ever belonged to such a club were to leave government service, Washington "would have the highest rate of unemployment of any city in the country."

During Nixon's period as President from 1969 to 1974, golf slowly began to take a back seat again. He showed up at Burning Tree somewhat regularly during his first term, usually with a supply of golf balls inscribed with his name and the presidential seal. Sometimes he gave one of them to a visitor with the admonition, "Use it only for putting. I wouldn't want someone to find it all cut up lying in the rough. He might think I hit it there."

Camera Shy

He also became increasingly shy about being photographed while golfing. In a memorandum to his aide Haldeman, written during the fall of the year he entered the White House, Nixon said that in Washington he would play only at Burning Tree because the club did not allow photographs to be taken on its course. Indeed, that became an edict: "Where clubs do allow photographs, I will not play there." He also instructed the Secret Service that he did not want to use caddies but preferred to play in a cart.

An important exception to the caddie rule applied in Japan, where Nixon found golf to be a unique experience. The female caddies there, he noted, "may not understand much English, but they are all great diplomats. Whenever you hit a ball, whether it goes in the bunker or out of bounds, they always say, 'good shot, good shot.' There is no better balm for a bruised ego."

Unlike some other Presidents who wanted all the help they could get, Nixon shunned gimme putts and was adamant about holing out. Burning Tree professional Elbin recalled one such occasion on the second green when Nixon actually scolded one of his opponents who wanted to concede a putt to him: "He said, 'No.

Don't give me the putt. Let me putt it out. I said I was going to learn to play this game.'"

As for keeping score, Nixon's reviews were contradictory. For example, Snead, in his autobiography, *Slammin' Sam*, told of playing with Nixon at The Greenbrier in White Sulphur Springs, West Virginia, and spotting what he believed to be an infraction of the rules: "He'd landed in some really bad rough that no one could shoot out of unless you had a bazooka. I was watching him from the fairway when he disappeared into the thicket. Hell, I thought he was going to drop another ball, take his loss in that situation and play on. But hell no—out comes his ball flyin' high onto the fairway. Then Nixon comes out of the woods looking real pleased with himself. I knew he threw it out, but what could I say. He was President."

It may well have been, of course, that Nixon actually found the ball and hit the recovery shot. He himself declined to comment on the incident. But Nixon had earlier made it clear that Snead was his favorite playing partner among the pros—"because he was such a great storyteller. He made me laugh so much I forgot how badly I was playing." Meanwhile, testimony from another of the President's occasional partners suggested that Snead may, indeed, have been mistaken about Nixon's shot. No less an authority than the Reverend Billy Graham praised Nixon at one of his religious crusades for, among other things, "his integrity in counting his golf score."

Graham's friendship with the President began in the early 1950s when, after being introduced by Senator Clyde Hoey of North Carolina, Nixon invited the noted evangelist for a game of golf. In later years, Graham on occasion flew to Nixon's secluded compounds in Florida and California, sometimes bringing along his chief lieutenant, Grady Wilson, for a round of golf. The fellowship on those private visits tended toward playfulness. The evangelist once noted that prayer never seemed to work for him on the golf course. "I think," he said, "it has something to do with my being a terrible putter." And after one game, which Wilson had won by holing a number of long putts, Nixon twitted him: "Greedy Grady. Greedy Grady. How's Greedy Grady, huh?"

Nixon was perhaps the most rabid sports fan of all Presidents. He liked to attend testimonial dinners for sports celebrities, and these ranged all the way from golfing great Bobby Jones to baseball manager Casey Stengel. Addressing a group of major-league baseball all-stars soon after he became President in 1969, Nixon said, "I am always awed in the presence of those who have made the team and are champions."

Nixon especially enjoyed the moments when sports teams were invited to the White House. Among them was the 1969 Ryder Cup team, which starred Dale Douglass, Frank Beard and Snead as nonplaying captain. And the President regularly telephoned winning players. For instance, when Orville Moody, fresh from a 14-year hitch in the army, won the 1969 U.S. Open at the Champions Golf Club in Houston, he received a congratulatory call from the President saying what a fine thing it was that somebody from the "middle class" had won the Open.

Nixon would travel coast to coast to attend a major football game. And when he couldn't be present, he would watch the New Year's bowl games simultaneously on separate television sets, again calling to congratulate the winning coaches. Not only that, he had an almost encyclopedic knowledge of sports figures and their statistics—batting and earned-run averages, pass-completion percentages, yards-per-carry and the like. Amateur psychologists of

Swinging in the Oval Office: Nixon gave a demonstration for golfer-comedian Bob Hope.

COURTESY, THE WHITE HOUSE

the day saw Nixon's preoccupation with sports as an escape into a realm where everything was black and white, with no moral judgments or motives to be questioned. But whatever the reason, said a friend, "It was astounding how thoroughly he read the sports pages. He always knew who was winning all the golf tournaments."

The President's golf outings grew rare during his abbreviated second term when the enormity of the Watergate crisis preoccupied him. He did, however, manage to get on the links while visiting Florida with his chum Charles G. "Bebe" Rebozo or while vacationing at what was known as the Summer White House at San Clemente, California. There, a group of local businessmen and financiers, calling themselves the Golfing Friends of the President, had commissioned the construction of a three-hole, nine-tee course (the longest hole was 220 yards) for him. After the course was completed in 1970, Nixon strolled around its fairways and occasionally took a few practice shots. But his daughter Julie and her husband, David Eisenhower, Ike's grandson, made greater use of the course when they visited San Clemente.

Leadership Question

Nixon was always touchy about the press, but never more so than during the Watergate period. He was concerned, he once said, that "occasionally some eager-beaver investigative reporter will count up the number of days the President is away and compare it to the time spent in Washington." He went so far as to quote President Theodore Roosevelt's warning to his successor, William Howard Taft, about the danger that his golf interests might suggest he was not taking the job with sufficient seriousness. But Nixon contended that the real measure of presidential leadership is how well a man makes decisions, not how long he sits at a desk. After one of Eisenhower's harrowing political ordeals, for example, Nixon reported seeing Ike by himself, pounding out 5-irons on the White House lawn. "That was his way," Nixon said, "of breaking the tension that might have devastated someone else."

The Back Nine: Recovering from a major operation in the lonely days after he resigned the presidency, Nixon found golf to be "my lifesaver." AP/WIDE WORLD PHOTOS

Yet it was only years later, in the aftermath of Watergate and a near-critical bout of phlebitis, that golf assumed a crucial importance in Nixon's life—that it became what he called "my lifesaver."

What happened was this: Shortly after his resignation and a major operation, Nixon found he was strong enough to swing a club again. Soon he began playing almost daily with Colonel Jack Brennan, who had been his top military aide during the last two years of his presidency and remained as his administrative assistant in San Clemente after the resignation. Brennan was not only an excellent golfer, he was also an understanding partner—as he had to be, Nixon said, since "out of practice and physically weak, I shot 125 the first time we played after leaving the hospital. I almost quit on the spot." But after a few months Nixon broke 100 and then 90, which pleased him so much that he kept the scorecards. Within a year, he reported, "I was shooting a few pars on the golf course and was back to par physically."

For all that, however, Nixon occasionally complained that golf could be a waste of time. "By the time you get dressed, drive out there, play 18 holes and come home, you've blown seven hours," he said. "There are better things you can do in that amount of time."

So finally, in his late 60s, he made the "hard decision" to give up the game. Why? For two reasons, Nixon explained. For one thing, he had a book deadline approaching; he felt he could not meet it and still find the time to play golf. For another, he noted, "One day in late 1978, I broke 80. I must admit it was on a relatively easy course . . . but for me it was like climbing Mount Everest. I knew I could never get any better, and so the competitive challenge was gone."

For a competitor like Richard Nixon, that was the clincher.

SPIRO AGNEW:
THE GREAT AMERICAN
DUFFER

While Richard Nixon often gave golf balls with the presidential seal and his name on them to playing partners, his first Vice President, Spiro T. Agnew, handed out much different golf balls. They featured a more modest legend, which said, "You have just been hit by. . . ." And Agnew would sign his name to them.

Such tokens were appropriate for Agnew (who resigned the vice presidency early in Nixon's second term after pleading no contest to a charge of income-tax evasion). Agnew developed an unhappy reputation at pro-am events for hitting wayward shots that struck spectators and, on one occasion, even a top professional with whom he was playing.

Agnew had taken up the game seriously when he was in his 40s and fairly promptly got his handicap down to 20—where it stayed. His wild shots inspired countless editorial cartoons showing galleries running for cover. And columnists wrote that it was not news when Agnew hit a spectator; on the contrary, it was news when he didn't hit a spectator.

Yet Agnew doggedly showed up at the Bob Hope Desert Classic in Palm Springs, California, while he was Vice President, and his description of the golfing challenge that presented could give pause even to low-handicappers. "I could see the thousands of people on either side of the tee . . . and extending down the fairway," he wrote in a bylined article, with John Underwood, for *Sports Illustrated*. One of his playing companions at this tournament in 1971 was baseball star Willie Mays, and Agnew was frightened, he confessed, when he saw how close Mays came to "those staring faces. I was aware of how vulnerable they were."

Agnew said that his initial impulse on the first tee was to tell the spectators to move back, and he waved for them to do that. But nobody budged. Then, he continued, "I teed the ball up. Waves of uncertainty swept through me. My legs were like jelly. I swayed coming into the shot, almost a lurch, and I clipped the ball with the toe of the club. It shot off to the right at a sharp angle, similar to a shank, but not with the power it would have carried had I hit it solidly with the open face. I knew I hit somebody. Actually it ricocheted off the arm of a man and hit his wife." Seeing the cameras, he instantly realized what was in store for him and had what he described as "a terrible sinking feeling."

Agnew went over to apologize to the woman he had hit and kissed her bruised forearm, and she told him to play on. He teed up another ball, thinking that it couldn't happen again. But he still felt shaky, with his legs weak and his head spinning. "Unbelievable as it seemed," he wrote, "I hit my second shot the same way, except this time much lower and a little harder." This one skipped through the gallery and hit a second woman on the ankle. He finished the round without any further incidents and with a fairly decent score after registering a number of pars (he was the only member of his foursome to par the 18th hole).

But then the Vice President learned that the second woman he'd hit had been taken to the hospital for observation. He sent her an autographed tray to make amends for her discomfort.

*Pro-Am Perils: Vice President
Agnew was noted for spraying
shots into galleries and once
beaned pro Doug Sanders
(rear) with an errant 3-wood
shot.* AP/WIDE WORLD PHOTOS

Agnew's most publicized wild shot, however, had occurred at
the previous year's Hope tournament when one of his wayward
3-woods beaned professional Doug Sanders and almost knocked
him out of the competition. The way Agnew told it, this time he
got off the first tee safely, if not effectively, by hooking his drive
some 150 yards past the line of spectators and onto a cart path.
"Sanders was in the fairway, ahead and to my right," he said. "The
crowd split, the bulk of it moving down to surround him and
shield him from my view."

The ground was hard and smooth, but his caddie handed him a
3-wood and then moved away. Agnew recalled that "I looked at the
club and the terrain and said to myself, 'I can't hit a 3-wood off
here, I need an iron.'" But there were so many people milling
around that he couldn't find his caddie again, so he hit the 3-wood
anyway and was absolutely correct about its being the wrong club.
"I came into the hard ground behind the ball," Agnew wrote, "and
pushed my shot to the right over the heads of the people surrounding

Sanders but, unfortunately, not over Sanders' head." The professional was gracious about the beaning, Agnew reported, got his head bandaged and continued with his round. Sanders won $200 in the tournament, Agnew said later, and that just paid for the medical attention he required.

In seeking to find reasons for his misadventures on the links, Agnew once described himself as "over-proed." He was seen, he felt, as an "active symbol of the great American duffer," the kind of player whom teaching professionals view as a challenging piece of raw material—whose grip might be moved a quarter turn to the right or the left to great advantage, whose stance might be narrowed or widened, whose backswing might be lengthened or shortened a bit. Yet the roles of all those teachers in his golfing life, he noted, were likened by the press to that of "the navigator of the *Titanic,* the intelligence aide of General Custer and the campaign manager of Harold Stassen."

CHAPTER 11

GERALD R. FORD

Duck, Here Comes the President

T here was a certain sense of sadness as well as resignation in the words of Gerald R. Ford as he reflected on one of the cruel ironies of his public years. "I think I'm as good an athlete," he said, "as anybody who's been in the White House."

Ford wasn't bragging. No other President had ever approached his impressive list of athletic credentials. As center and a captain of the University of Michigan football teams in the middle 1930s—days when participants played both offense and defense—Ford was a standout and was selected for the squad of collegiate all-stars that met the professional Chicago Bears in 1935. He even received bids to play professional football from the Green Bay Packers and the Detroit Lions. Ford turned down those offers, but went on to coach both football and boxing to help work his way through law school and became an expert skier and a popular participant in pro-am golf events.

Yet you wouldn't have known he was an accomplished athlete—not from the way the President of the United States from 1974 to 1977 was portrayed on television and in the press. Ford was depicted as a bumbling, uncoordinated man who had stumbled his way onto the world stage (as he once did coming off an airplane on an official visit to Europe). Newspapers featured pictures of Ford when he took tumbles on the ski slopes or tried to hit his golf ball

The Power of the Presidency: Ford was a big, strong man with an impressive shoulder turn that produced a mighty swing. But spectators sometimes had to take cover.

AP/WIDE WORLD PHOTOS

out of improbable lies in trees or bushes. And countless articles were published describing how Ford had peppered the galleries with wild shots during golf tournaments.

No one got more mileage out of poking fun at Ford's erratic golf game than entertainer Bob Hope. The politician and the comedian golfed together as often as 20 times a year, which gave Hope such insights into Ford's game as the following:

- "Jerry Ford has made golf a contact sport. He's the most dangerous driver since Ben Hur."
- "Ford doesn't really have to keep score; he can just look back and count the wounded."
- "One of my most prized possessions is the Purple Heart I received for all the golf I've played with him."
- "You can recognize him on the course because his golf cart has a red cross painted on the top."

- "The Russians used to say that if we were really serious about disarmament, we'd dismantle his golf clubs."

The truth of the matter was that Ford's golf game bore little resemblance to the way it was described. Despite the unflattering press, Ford was the first President who had the confidence to put his game on public display by playing in pro-am tournaments when he was in the White House. He didn't even mind being featured on telecasts of the events, from the Pebble Beach links in California to Doral in Florida, playing with leading professionals of the time. And he was particularly proud of a 40-foot putt he holed on the final green of the 1977 Bob Hope Desert Classic that was captured for posterity on television.

There were two sides to such appearances, however. On the one hand, Ford genuinely enjoyed the competition, and his presence drew thousands of extra spectators to the huge galleries that lined the fairways at these events—adding markedly to the coffers of the charities that benefited from them. On the other hand, the immense crowds that gathered around the President constituted a special hazard, one that Ford called "intimidating, especially if you have any tendencies to be a little erratic." The almost-inevitable result led to all the publicity about his errant shots ricocheting off spectators.

Ford, who stressed that he was by no means the only person ever to bean spectators, said he struggled to become "immune" to the huge galleries, trying his best "to keep from hitting lousy shots." And much of the time he succeeded. A tall, powerfully built man, he was capable of cracking exceptionally long drives. At the 1974 opening of the World Golf Hall of Fame in Pinehurst, North Carolina, for instance, the President's initial tee shot traveled about 270 yards, outdistancing those of such fellow competitors as Arnold Palmer and Gary Player. On that day, only Jack Nicklaus outdrove the President and only by about 20 yards. "Distance isn't my problem," Ford admitted. "It's direction."

Ford's swing, while quite functional, was no thing of beauty, in part because of knee injuries he suffered on the gridiron and

On the Tee with the Big Three: At the 1974 opening of the World Golf Hall of Fame in Pinehurst, North Carolina, Jack Nicklaus outdrove Ford. But Arnold Palmer (left) and Gary Player (right) didn't. AP/WIDE WORLD PHOTOS

aggravated while skiing (he eventually had knee-joint replacement surgery). His stance was rather flat-footed and his backswing long and deliberately slow. The club almost appeared to move in slow motion. At the same time, he had a big shoulder turn and brought his hands through powerfully, which accounted for his length off the tee. But his short game was inconsistent, and from time to time he went through long spells of putting woes.

Still, Ford was a true golf nut—he virtually retired from the White House to the links—and if his game failed to live up to his commitment to the sport, that can be said about a lot of people. The fact is, what was an eminently respectable game when he was younger held up exceptionally well in his later years. As a youth, Ford's handicap had dipped as low as 12, and during his White House years it hovered around 18. Even when he was in his late 70s, his handicap fluctuated in the 15 to 17 range. Ford may never have experienced the joy of breaking 80 (his best score was an 81 at the Cascades course at The Homestead in Hot Springs, Virginia), but he could boast of three holes-in-one, all made after he left the White House.

Friendly and outwardly easygoing, Ford seemed to shrug off all the publicity about clobbering spectators. "If you're going to be in the public eye," the President declared, "you have to expect the press to do what they think is a good line that is not very complimentary."

Underneath, however, the constant harping rankled. He admitted that "the portrayal of me as an oafish ex-jock made for good copy" but found it "hard to take." "I developed a good exterior posture," Ford once wrote of the way he was portrayed. "The truth of the matter is that some of my favorite pipes have teeth marks in their stems that you wouldn't believe."

Toting the Bag

The President was initiated into the game as a caddie. When Ford was in his early teens, his stepfather took up golf at what was then the Masonic Country Club in their hometown of Grand Rapids, Michigan, and young Gerald was occasionally pressed into service carrying clubs. "If I had caddied on a regular basis," he later admitted ruefully, "my game today would be a lot better."

After he enrolled at the University of Michigan, as Ford told it, his sporting life was dominated by football. When he graduated in 1935 and chose not to play professionally, Michigan coach Harry Kipke recommended him for a job coaching freshman football and boxing at Yale. Once he got to New Haven, he found he had plenty of spare time, so he started playing at the famous Yale course designed by American golfing pioneer Charles B. MacDonald. Before long, Ford could claim a handicap of about 12. But after he was admitted to Yale law school, he put his clubs aside and didn't pick them up again until he had graduated.

Ford returned to Grand Rapids and set up a law practice with a classmate, Philip Buchen, who later served as his White House counsel, but found that "during the first year we were not overwhelmed with business." So in the spring of 1941—and at a cost

Caddie Days: Ford's introduction to the game came as a youngster when he was asked to carry clubs for his stepfather in Grand Rapids, Michigan.

COURTESY, THE GERALD R. FORD LIBRARY

of $100—he joined the Kent Country Club, a 6,514-yard layout he described as "an old and very nice" country club. "I could leave the office at 5:30," he said, "and play 18 holes. I was single and had a lot of time." And again, as had happened at Yale, he reported a handicap of about 12.

Any further progress was interrupted by World War II and the subsequent birth of his political career. Returning to Michigan after four years serving in the Pacific with the navy, he courted and married his wife, Betty, started a family and, as he put it, "got interested in politics." Ford was elected to Congress in 1949 as a

Republican and didn't resume golf with any degree of commitment until he became House minority leader in 1965, the year in which he also joined the Burning Tree Club in Maryland.

The long layoff took its toll. While Ford managed to play about once a week in those days and generally shot in the neighborhood of bogey golf, the basic pattern of his game was in place. He was long off the tee, but his short game, as Burning Tree professional Max Elbin put it, "failed to do him justice. And he couldn't putt for sour apples."

Then, in 1973, the first in a series of events that would shake the Republic to its foundation changed life dramatically for Gerald Ford. Incumbent Vice President Spiro Agnew resigned from office after pleading no contest to a charge of income-tax evasion, and Richard M. Nixon reached into the Congress to tap the minority leader as Vice President. The duties of that office hardly diminished Ford's enthusiasm for golf. He even played three or four times with Nixon, who, he said, performed "reasonably well"—although he said he didn't remember the results of the matches.

Otherwise, Ford continued to play as often as he could. An old Washington gag has it that anyone looking for a game would do well to call the Vice President; in any administration, he's the one person who's most likely to have nothing to do. Actually, Ford had a fairly full plate as Vice President, with a work schedule that would have tested the ingenuity of even the most dedicated golfer.

Take the time in late July 1974, when he had promised one of his golfing pals, Congressman Thomas "Tip" O'Neill of Massachusetts, that he would play with him in a pro-am at the Pleasant Valley Classic in Sutton, Massachusetts. Ford's schedule called for him to fly to Washington from San Diego, California, catch three hours' sleep, then hop on another plane to arrive in time for the golf tournament in Massachusetts. When he reached Washington, however, he discovered that he had to substitute for President Nixon at a ceremony honoring a military officer.

Ford barely broke stride: He presented the medal, rushed home to change his clothes and snoozed for an hour and a half on the plane. "Anyone else would have been traveling on one cylinder," reported a sponsor of the event, "but he was charged up to play. He hit balls for photographers for about 10 minutes, shook enough hands in the gallery to weaken the average grip and then teed off on schedule."

Barely a week later, as the Watergate scandal stumbled toward its conclusion, Nixon himself resigned the presidency—and Gerald Ford suddenly found himself in the White House. Among the myriad problems confronting the new President, there was even a small golfing one: He had promised to attend that opening of the Professional Golfers' Association's World Golf Hall of Fame in Pinehurst in early September.

Remarkably, considering the unprecedented political turmoil that was sweeping the nation's capital, Ford kept his promise. He headed for North Carolina a mere 72 hours after pardoning his predecessor for any crimes that might have been associated with Watergate—the most controversial act of his presidency, but one he justified as crucial to helping the nation get over its long political nightmare.

Ford had invited Burning Tree's Elbin to ride along on Air Force One; he even asked the pro to edit the text of the remarks he was to give to correct any potential mistakes in golfing lore. (Elbin related that he cut out a reference to a famous woman professional playing at Burning Tree, a course restricted to male members.) And after what *Golf* magazine called "a stirring in the crowd and craning of necks as additional Secret Service men moved into place," Elbin emerged first, looking slightly embarrassed. "Boy, that's class," noted one bystander. "Who else would think of bringing his home pro to a party like this?" Finally, Ford followed, as a band played "Hail to the Chief."

It was suggested that one of the reasons Ford decided to go to North Carolina was that the increasingly reclusive Ben Hogan was also due to attend. "He must know how hard it is to get Ben Hogan out of Texas," said one Pinehurst official. In any event, the President sat next to Hogan on the dais during the ceremonies following the day's golf. And while many of the assembled golfing officials and PGA members still buzzed about his long drive at the first tee, Ford put the day's events in perspective: "This afternoon for a few hours, quite unsuccessfully, I tried to make a hole-in-one," he said. "Tomorrow morning, I'll be back in Washington trying to get out of one."

Just Jerry

Despite his lofty new responsibilities, Ford generally tried to remain one of the boys when he was on the links. Many playing companions reported that when they called him "Mr. President," in deference to his new office, he would counsel them, "Out here, I'm just Jerry Ford." According to one longtime Burning Tree member, the President would arrive at the club "like any other member and pick up a game with anyone who's ready to go. He just goes out there and has a hell of a good time." He kept his old locker on the main floor of the clubhouse, and, as Elbin put it, "He was just the same. He went into the clubhouse, and if you wanted to speak to him about something, he'd put that foot up on the bench and talk to you like you were his friend."

Ford was equally open with members of the White House staff, quite in contrast to some of his predecessors who preferred more formality. First Lady Betty Ford wrote in her memoirs that the President frequently exchanged golf scores with the White House butler. Indeed, veteran professional Gene Sarazen, who played with many golfing Presidents dating back to Warren G. Harding, once expressed the view that Ford had the same kind of personal charm that Dwight D. Eisenhower did. When someone remarked that it was difficult to be a hero in the White House in the post-Watergate era, Sarazen added, "Yes, but this fellow's a big hitter. And all the world loves a big hitter."

Sarazen rated Ford as the best striker of the ball of any of the Presidents he had played with, but more remarkable was his dedication to the game. "I've seen him play in snow and rain, with a cold, and he wouldn't quit," said Sanford Weill, a Wall Street executive and longtime playing companion. "His knees were hurting, but he'd go into deep traps and then go on to the next hole, putting it all behind him. You're talking about a man who absolutely loves the game."

As anyone who has played golf learns, however, such affection can be sorely tested by the frustrations of the game. And so it was with Ford, who on occasion could exhibit major displays of temper. As Wall Streeter Weill put it, when asked if Ford slammed clubs into the ground: "Not too often." And did he swear? "Is he not human?" Weill responded. The President's mood swings, not surprisingly, often depended on how he was faring on the course. When he was winning, he was likely to be friendly and affable; when he was behind, even his Secret Service aides learned to keep their distance.

Rodney Markley, a Ford Motor Company vice president, remembered a golfing vacation he and the President took along with two of Ford's other best golfing buddies, William Whyte of U.S. Steel and San Diego manufacturer Leon Parma. At the end, the group awarded special trophies. The President's was for "longest putter throw," based on his response to a short putt he had missed. "Sometimes the air is blue when he gets mad at himself on the golf course," Markley recalled. "But the anger is directed at himself— and most of the time he is in control of his temper."

Ford's temperamental tendencies surfaced early in his golfing career. Once, while on a trip home from his job at Yale, he made a visit to the links that became the stuff of family legend. It seems one of his younger brothers was emerging as something of an athlete, and Ford was asked to take the boy out for a round of golf— and a lecture about sportsmanship and playing the game for its own sake. Ford felt he was making progress until his own game fell apart on the 17th tee; he dribbled his tee shot, whiffed the next one and then ripped off a 90-degree slice. He then wrapped his driver around the tee box. "See," Ford told his admiring younger brother. "Nobody can win all the time."

A more public example of the Ford temper occurred during the Bing Crosby National Pro-Am tournament at Pebble Beach one time when the President was teamed with Arnold Palmer. Ford had played fairly well. But then, according to Richard Wammock, a PGA official who for years was responsible for the President's security during pro-am events, he "began hitting the ball everywhere.

On the 18th he whips his tee shot right into the ocean. Then, shooting 3, he smacks it down the fairway. Then he flubs his fourth shot." His anger was apparent to all, and no one dared approach him. "I just happened to walk by," Wammock told a reporter for *Golf Digest,* "and he turns to me and says, 'You can just tell [host Bing Crosby] to take me out of this thing next year. I will not be back.'" Of course, within an hour the President had calmed down—and he did return the following year.

Beyond sheer competitiveness, another reason for the President's intensity was that his games usually involved money. The wagers were not the huge ones favored by some of his celebrity partners; nassaus in the two- to five-dollar range were typical. "I don't enjoy playing for big stakes," Ford once said. "I've never been a gambler." But the President often acted as if billions in federal aid were on the line. As one partner described it, "The man hates to part with money. He'll pay you when he loses, but boy he hates it, and he says, 'O.K., when are we going to play again?'"

Picking Up the Pace

A result was that the Ford foursomes would sometimes fall behind the pace of play in pro-am events, and it was the job of the PGA's Wammock to make sure that the players speeded up. "I'd have to walk up to him and say, 'Mr. President, we're behind. You've got to play faster.' Sometimes he'd say, 'Fine, let's get going,' and other times it would be things you can't print. He'd stare at me with those cold blue eyes, but he'd speed up."

The President's intensity also could have a more playful side. In addition to calling all the usual instructions to a ball after he had hit it—"bite!"; "get up!"; and the like—he would direct an occasional barb at one of his companions. While playing in Vail with economist Alan Greenspan, for example, he expressed a little surprise when the chairman of his Council of Economic Advisers uncorked a particularly long and straight drive. "I see you haven't been studying those charts all the time," he said.

Missing Voters: Ford drew huge galleries when he played in the Bing Crosby tournament after losing the 1976 presidential race. His reaction: "Where were all these people on Election Day?" UPI/BETTMANN

Ford's presidency ended in 1977, after he narrowly lost the election to Jimmy Carter, a nongolfer (see chapter 15). While the shift of national power hasn't always been conducted with good grace (John Quincy Adams, for instance, didn't even attend his successor's inauguration), Ford shook his rival's hand warmly after his swearing-in ceremony. But he didn't stick around any longer than he had to. Almost immediately, he departed by helicopter, then flew to Pebble Beach and teed off in the Bing Crosby pro-am tournament.

The newly anointed ex-President teamed up with Palmer, attracting one of the largest galleries ever seen at a PGA event, according to an official who drove what he called "the getaway car" for Ford (it included a Secret Service agent with a green case, inside of which was a submachine gun). At one point, another PGA official was heard to remark, "If everybody out here tries to go to the 18th hole with Ford, it'll sink."

The President's reaction?

"Where were all these people on Election Day?"

To cap things off, he delighted the crowd by chipping in for a birdie 4 on Pebble's difficult uphill 14th hole.

While Ford kept one eye on the political arena—there were reports that he might run for office again in 1980—he embarked upon a golfing schedule that led one golf publication to suggest that he might wind up the year playing in more events than Jack Nicklaus. In addition to the Crosby, Ford participated in pro-am events all across the country, including the Jackie Gleason Inverrary Classic in Fort Lauderdale, Florida; the Sammy Davis Jr. Hartford Open in Connecticut; and the Dinah Shore tournament, a major stop on the Ladies' PGA tour.

Later that year, at what was then called the Danny Thomas Memphis Classic, Ford scored his first hole-in-one. The circumstances were best summarized in a poem Ford wrote in response to a congratulatory note from professional Dave Stockton, with whom he had been paired earlier in Tip O'Neill's Massachusetts pro-am. It read as follows:

> Dear Dave,
> 'Twas the Danny Thomas Memphis Classic
> on Wednesday, June the eighth,
> The fifth hole and a 5-iron shot
> was flying true and straight.
> A hole-in-one, the golfer's dream
> for me had now come true.
> That thrill is sweeter yet because
> a note has come from you.

Ford signed off by saying he appreciated the pro's congratulations "on my big day."

Stockton, a two-time PGA champion and later captain of the victorious 1991 U.S. Ryder Cup team, had the poem laminated and put it on the wall of his home in Mentone, California.

Ford eventually settled in Rancho Mirage, California, near Palm Springs, building a house on a golf course. This area of California is a golfing mecca, and it allowed Hope, another resident, to toss off yet one more of his caustic observations about the President's golf game: "There are over 50 courses in Palm Springs, and he never knows which one he'll play until he hits his first drive."

Yet on one of those courses, the 6,862-yard Tamarisk Country Club, Ford scored two more holes-in-one, two years apart—both of them made with a 5-iron and both of them on the 174-yard 11th hole. "It's amazing," Ford said of the coincidence, and then added, "I've had trouble with [that hole] since."

A Tournament of His Own

At this point, the President began spending more time at Vail, where there were both challenging golf courses and ski slopes. Then one day, while chatting with his chief of staff, Bob Barrett, and some local businessmen, he came up with the idea of having a pro-am of his own, the Jerry Ford Invitational. The idea was to promote golf in Vail "because it is so beautiful up there in the Rocky Mountains," as he put it. And Ford invited people he knew from the golfing and entertainment worlds—as well as a number of other amateurs. The tournament, which Ford called "the most satisfying thing I have ever done in the game," raised more than $1 million in its first 15 years for local charities—ranging from scholarships for poor children to support for ham radio operators who help coordinate mountain rescue operations in the winter.

Ford, meanwhile, continued to work on his own game. Many of the professionals with whom he played gave him pointers—which, as most such suggestions seem to do, helped on a temporary basis. He used a mixed set of clubs—some from Nicklaus, some from Ping and even some Kenneth Smith woods and irons. He was particularly pleased with a Ping L-shaped wedge he acquired and that he said "helped a lot in getting out of the sand."

But putting was something else again, and the short stick continued to plague him. The President contended that he had been a pretty good putter at one time—"but then all of a sudden I got the yips, like a lot of older people do." Eventually, he adopted a longer putter—a 45-inch one designed to be held against the lower part of the chest and propelled in a pendulum motion by a pincer grip with the right hand. He saw his putting "improve a lot." Purists might decry the use of this weapon, but Ford explained that he had played with Arnold Palmer when the golfing legend was using a long putter (he later went back to a more orthodox one), "and I figured if Arnold could use it, I should."

As Ford approached his 80th birthday, he gradually began to wind down his extensive pro-am schedule. Where he had once thought nothing of a coast-to-coast trip for a golf tournament, he said, he started "cutting back on all kinds of travel, period." For Ford, that meant only about half a dozen such events a year, including his own tournament, most of them near where he lived. He made the decision somewhat regretfully, he admitted, because "good [charitable] causes, good people"—not geography—had always been his criteria in selecting events. "But today, at my age, I just don't like to travel that much anymore."

Trouble Shot: The press delighted in printing pictures of Ford playing out of improbable lies, such as this photo taken in Vail, Colorado.
AP/WIDE WORLD PHOTOS

Yet through it all, Ford remained very much the devoted golfer and golfing fan that he had been for years—so much so that he became one of only a handful of golfers ever selected as honorary lifetime members of the Professional Golfers' Association. For the 1994 premiere of the Presidents Cup, which pitted top American professionals against their international counterparts, he was tapped as the honorary chairman of the event. And he continued to telephone pros to congratulate them on their victories—which he followed shot by shot on television. Hope, in his book, *Confessions of a Hooker,* related that Ford was particularly impressed after seeing Tom Watson edge Jack Nicklaus by chipping in for a birdie 2 on the 17th hole to win the 1982 Open at Pebble Beach.

"Listen," Hope told him, "that ball only traveled 27 feet. I hit lots of shots 27 feet. Sometimes with my driver."

"Yes, but do you realize the ball went 27 feet without hitting anybody?" the President responded—or so Hope said he did.

Unfortunately, his reputation for erratic play was something Gerald Ford was never quite able to shake. But at least he was able to repay his most constant critic in kind. "Although you have taken some license in ridiculing my golf game before large audiences," he once told Hope, "I am nevertheless proud that you treat me in a manner equal to that of other Presidents you have known, such as Teddy Roosevelt, James Polk and Andy Jackson."

CHAPTER 12

RONALD REAGAN
The Gipper Goes Golfing

To judge by press accounts published during his White House years, Ronald Reagan was a horseman; he even wanted to ride his favorite steed, El-Alamein, down Pennsylvania Avenue after his inauguration, until the Secret Service intervened. He was a fitness addict; his daily weight-lifting regime was widely publicized. And he was an outdoorsman; he enjoyed chopping wood and digging holes for fence posts at Rancho del Cielo, his California retreat.

But a golfer? Not so you'd notice. About the only sign of Reagan's involvement in the game came each New Year's Eve, when newspapers duly reported that he played what he referred to as his "annual round" at Sunnylands, the Rancho Mirage, California, home of Walter Annenberg, the publishing magnate and one-time U.S. ambassador to the United Kingdom.

Each year the President and a few of his cronies, often including Secretary of State George Shultz, would get together for "a few days of parties, socializing with friends, wonderful meals—and, yes, a bit of golf," as the President described it. On occasion the golfing portion even embraced famous professionals, as was the case late in Reagan's presidential years when Tom Watson and Lee Trevino were asked to join in. As Watson recalled the incident, he was in

Annual Outing: Each New Year's Eve, Reagan played at the California course of publisher Walter Annenberg (second from left). In 1988, they were joined by Secretary of State George Shultz and pros Lee Trevino and Tom Watson. COURTESY, THE RONALD REAGAN LIBRARY

California for a preseason tune-up and vacation with his family and was taking a shower when Trevino telephoned to report the invitation. Watson's wife, Linda, relayed the classic "Guess who you're playing golf with tomorrow" message. For the match, Reagan was given a "generous" but undisclosed handicap and teamed with Trevino against Watson and Shultz, a 12-handicapper. The President boomed his drive off the first tee, but the Reagan-Trevino team was one hole down when they reached the par-4 18th. There, Reagan dropped a six-foot putt to square the match. "The President finally holed a putt," Watson said with a big grin.

Yet the longevity of the gathering at Annenberg's course—it eventually became a tradition of some four decades' duration—reflected the little-known fact that Reagan had much more than a passing interest in golf. Reagan's White House years (1981 to

1989) represented a modest lull in his pursuit of the royal and ancient game. He was the only golfing President since Dwight D. Eisenhower, for instance, who didn't play at the Burning Tree Club and other top courses in the Washington area.

But at other times in his life—as a young actor in Hollywood, as a television spokesman for corporate America and after he left Washington—he got serious about the game and played considerably more often. "When I became President," as he put it, "my golf game took a dramatic nosedive."

That comment applied to quality as well as to frequency. Not only did Reagan always enjoy what he called "the friendly competition," there was a time when he could more than hold his own on the links. "Although I say this modestly," he declared, "my game was pretty good." How good? According to the best reports, his handicap was as low as 12 in his prepolitical days. And even as he approached the age of 80, his swing—if not his scores—showed signs of the game he once played. After their round at the Annenberg course, for instance, Trevino observed that the President was a big, strong man and that he hit some shots of which anyone could have been proud. As one of the frequent playing partners of Reagan's later years sized up his game: "It's obvious when you see him hit the ball that at one time he played a lot and was an excellent golfer."

Stone-Age Start

The way the President told it, "I've been playing golf practically since the Stone Age. During my youth, however, I probably spent more time carrying clubs than actually swinging them." While he was in high school in Dixon, Illinois, he and a number of his friends earned "a little extra money" by caddieing at the town's country club. But Reagan preferred working as a lifeguard at Lowell Park, a popular swimming spot on the Rock River, where, according to contemporary accounts, he became something of a local hero by saving no fewer than 77 lives during the six summers that he worked there. They were, he said years later, "some of the most glorious months of my life." He also was able to save the $400 he needed

Customer Golf: During his days as a corporate spokesman, Reagan had plenty of time to work on grooving his swing. COURTESY, THE RONALD REAGAN LIBRARY

to pay for his first year at Eureka College in Peoria, Illinois, with earnings from his jobs as a caddie and a lifeguard.

The young Reagan was a sports fanatic and often spoke to friends about his dream of becoming a star athlete. But rather than golf, he said, "as a young boy I concentrated on football and swimming instead." "Dutch" Reagan, as he was known in those days (the nickname was bestowed upon him as a baby by his father), played football in both high school and college—though because of his extreme nearsightedness he was relegated to a guard position. He excelled at swimming; at one meet during his freshman year at Eureka, he won every event except the breaststroke. He also ran track, became a campus leader (spearheading a student strike) and starred in a number of plays for the Eureka Dramatic Club. It was all a portent of the pursuits that shaped his later life. He once said his interests lay in "drama, sports and politics—and not always in that order."

After graduating from Eureka, Reagan talked his way into a job as a sportscaster for a local radio station, capitalizing on his knowledge of football and a dramatic flair for detail. Eventually he wound up at a Des Moines, Iowa, station where he made a name for himself announcing Chicago Cubs baseball games. He was especially adept at reconstructing action on the field from telegraph reports. That skill proved particularly useful one day when the ticker went dead for more than six minutes; Reagan deftly filled in the air time by having the Cubs' Augie Galan foul off pitch after pitch from Dizzy Dean of the St. Louis Cardinals until service was resumed. In 1937, Reagan followed the Cubs to spring training in California, made a screen test, and soon Dutch Reagan, sportscaster, became Ronald Reagan, actor.

Cooperative Climate

In Hollywood Reagan had "more opportunities to play" golf than ever before, and "in sunny California I found the weather to be much more cooperative." He described his situation this way: "As an actor for Warner Brothers, I was always occupied making one picture or another, and golf was a relaxing way to spend a weekend afternoon."

The first club Reagan joined in California was the Lakeside Golf Club in Burbank, where one member recalled that "he never got to play a lot but he did have about an 18 handicap." Reagan's membership at that club, however, produced something of a controversy. Not long after being admitted in 1941, he discovered that Lakeside, like many clubs of the day, "was strictly enforcing discriminatory practices—racial and religious. That type of policy was something that I simply could not condone, so I quickly sent off a rather strong letter, urging them to abolish those policies. I remember telling them that in America such exclusion should not be tolerated." He also felt strongly that "I should withdraw my membership immediately." Later, Reagan learned that "my typewritten letter was hung on the wall at the club, and many of the members and staff used it as a dart board."

Subsequently, Reagan played at the Hillcrest Country Club in Los Angeles, to which a number of actors belonged, and enjoyed games with other Hollywood golfing types, including Jack Benny and George Burns. Moreover, he often used the breaks between making pictures for golfing holidays. Actress Jane Wyman, his wife from 1940 to 1948, also liked the game and sometimes joined him on the links. Nancy Reagan, his second wife, was not a golfer.

In all, Reagan acted in 54 motion pictures during his Holly-wood career, working his way up from low-budget B movies and westerns (using his abilities as a horseman) to roles in some major motion pictures. He even made a short film called *Shoot Yourself Some Golf,* with long-hitter Jimmy Thomson, which cast Reagan as a duffer getting some pointers from Thomson.

His most memorable role, however, came in *Knute Rockne—All-American.* That was the film in which he played the part of George Gipp, a fabled Notre Dame football star who died while still in school. Reagan's role involved his running 80 yards for a touchdown in front of a wildly cheering crowd and a deathbed scene in which he told Pat O'Brien, who played Rockne, "Someday, when things are tough, maybe you can tell the boys to go in there and win just once for the Gipper." The movie served two functions: It enabled Reagan to realize his childhood fantasy of athletic stardom, at least vicariously, and it won him the lasting nickname, the Gipper.

After World War II, during which Reagan spent much of his time making training films for the army and navy, he served several terms as president of the Screen Actors Guild, eventually negotiating a new contract with the studios that resulted in better pay and benefits for the members. Then in 1954 he became the television host for *General Electric Theater,* with duties involving speaking at GE factories and various civic groups around the country.

It was during the eight years he spent as a spokesman for General Electric that Reagan later claimed he was at his peak as a golfer. "When I hit the speaking circuit," he explained, "I found that my schedule was flexible enough to work in regular golf games." One professional who played with him in those days recalled that he had a powerful, if somewhat wristy, swing—"and the prettiest set of Tommy Armour clubs you could ever imagine." As he traveled around the nation on behalf of GE—meeting with executives and their clients—he managed to play often enough to get his handicap down to 12. But after that, Reagan related, his game "was all downhill" as he went on to serve two terms as governor of California and to move into the White House.

How to Throw a Club

Playing golf may have taken a back seat during Reagan's political years, but his clubs still stood at the ready. En route to the Geneva summit conference in 1986, for instance, he demonstrated his putting prowess in the aisle of Air Force One before a high-powered audience that included Secretary of State Shultz and Chief of Staff Donald Regan as well as a photographer. Golfing images

Airborne Shot: Staffers watched as Reagan displayed his putting stroke aboard Air Force One.

AP/WIDE WORLD PHOTOS

also crept into his comments quite frequently. A White House aide described how, on one of the relatively rare occasions when he lost his temper, the President threw a pencil across the room and then quipped, "I learned a long time ago that if you're going to throw a club in anger, throw it in front of you so you won't have to go back and pick it up." And he had a stock reply when anyone wanted to know his handicap: "Congress."

Such banter and anecdotes were the hallmark of Reagan's personality. They seemed to have had their genesis in heredity—but the golf course played a role, too. The President explained it this way: One of his fondest childhood memories was of walking with his father, Jack Reagan, on the links in Dixon, "where he and a few of his buddies would play." Reagan called those occasions "a special time" and said he especially enjoyed listening to his father "tell stories to the other fellows. He was blessed with the remarkable gift of storytelling and used to enjoy making the guys laugh."

The President had the same gift. Throughout his life, Reagan was an amiable playing partner who quickly put people at ease by spinning yarns that could be amusing, witty or sometimes even slightly ribald. One that he particularly fancied, for example, was a variation on the old joke about the American golfer on vacation in Ireland. The golfer, a hopeless duffer, hacked his way around course after course until one day he sliced a ball into the woods next to a big toadstool, upon which a leprechaun was perched.

"How's it going?" the leprechaun asked.

"Terrible," responded the American, "and I'd give anything to be able to play this game."

"That can be arranged," the leprechaun said, explaining that he could make the American an excellent golfer but that his sex life would be negatively affected.

After pondering the offer for a split second, the visitor agreed, chipped his ball back into the fairway and parred the hole—along with every remaining one on the course. He returned to America to win his club championship, a regional amateur title and just about every other tournament in sight.

The next year the American visited Ireland again and, for the first time since his last visit, sliced the ball—which wound up in the woods next to the same leprechaun sitting on the same toadstool.

"Well," said the leprechaun, "How has your year been?"

"Fantastic," replied the American. "I won my club championship and some other titles and I think I may qualify for the Open this year."

"That's not what I meant," the leprechaun said. "How many times have you been with a woman in the last year?"

"Four," replied the American, after a moment's thought.

"Four?" echoed the leprechaun. "That's nothing to brag about."

"It's not bad for a priest in a small town in Iowa," shrugged the American.

Like many Presidents, Reagan relished the visits of sports figures to the White House and often managed to make the

On the Dance Floor: When U.S. Open champion Raymond Floyd visited the Oval Office in 1986, Reagan gave him a unique demonstration of putting form.

COURTESY, THE RONALD REAGAN LIBRARY

ceremonies fairly lighthearted. After Raymond Floyd won the U.S. Open in 1986, the President used the occasion to get a few putting tips and grimaced wildly when the ball failed to go where he wanted. He delighted the members of the 1987 New York Giants football team, when they showed up in the Rose Garden after their Super Bowl victory, by dumping a Gatorade bucket over linebacker Harry Carson, just as Carson had done to coach Bill Parcells (this time, though, the bucket was filled with popcorn).

Toward the end of his White House years, Reagan threw out the first ball at a baseball game at Wrigley Field for the Chicago Cubs, whose contests he had announced as a young man. He then went into the broadcast booth and called one-and-a-half innings of play-by-play. The President began his broadcast by saying, "In a few months I'll be out of a job, so I thought I'd audition here."

Relearning Process

He needn't have worried. Reagan was much in demand as a speaker in his post-White House years. But if he was in good form on the rostrum, his golf swing was in need of repair. As he put it, "I've had to take some lessons to relearn much of what was automatic in my earlier years." Ed Oldfield Jr., then the head professional at the Los Angeles Country Club, was the teacher he turned to first, and Oldfield called the President "a very good student. He tries hard, and he'll do what you tell him to." Although Oldfield said "right now we don't keep score too much," he observed that Reagan had the potential to be "someone who breaks 90."

In contrast to his once-a-year games at Walter Annenberg's estate, Reagan began playing once a week—sometimes even more frequently. Most often he played at the Los Angeles Country Club, where he had an honorary membership and "which is near my home and office." And while he still golfed with Hollywood types (actor Tom Selleck was a frequent partner), he developed "a close circle of friends that I enjoy playing with on a regular basis," including companions from the business and financial worlds. His foursomes varied "depending on their schedules and mine, but, heck, I'll play with anybody who's willing—as long as they don't take the game too seriously."

The President wasn't kidding. Those outings, which generally consisted of lunch followed by nine holes of golf, were described as "very relaxed" by several of the participants—at least as relaxed as such games could be with Reagan's contingent of Secret Service agents lurking about. In fact, the Los Angeles club's members were a bit concerned when the President was offered honorary membership, but the agents turned out to be "quite friendly people," according to one member, and never disrupted play at all.

After lunch—during which Reagan usually amused his companions with stories about politics and golf—the players teed off around 1:30 P.M. and, "making sure that we don't hold anyone up," finished at about 4:00 P.M. (he generally skipped the 19th hole and went directly home in a waiting automobile). The President was granted "permanent" honors—a tradition Annenberg had instituted for the New Years' outings—and got to tee off first at each hole. "He's kind of embarrassed by it," reported Chase Morsey, one of his frequent companions, "but it's a courtesy afforded him because of the job he held."

The weekly sessions were more informal and social than fiercely fought. Reagan remained competitive on the course but seemed genuinely pleased if one of his playing partners did well. "If you hit a good shot," said Thomas "Tuck" Trainer, "it's like he hit a good shot." And his sense of humor remained very much in evidence. He got some metal woods, for instance, and initially he couldn't hit them at all. After one unfortunate miscue, the President turned to Trainer and said, "I think I know what I'm going to do with them. I'm going to melt them down and make an ashtray out of them— and, Tuck, I don't smoke."

The President continued to practice, though not usually on days when he had a game. His wife, Nancy, gave him a new set of clubs and a maroon golf bag, and he was reported to have become particularly adroit with the 5-wood, especially in getting out of the rough. Like any golfer, from time to time he suffered all the game's worst indignities, but on occasion he'd hole a 30-foot putt or hit a

Presidential Pairing: To reporters and photographers watching a game Reagan played with his successor, George Bush (left), the former actor offered an excuse ahead of time: "I'm camera shy." COURTESY, THE RONALD REAGAN LIBRARY

magnificent shot. One of his most memorable occurred on the 185-yard par-3 fifth hole at the South Course at the Los Angeles Country Club. Reagan put his tee shot about pin high—but in a cavernous sand trap to the left of the green. From where he stood in the bunker, he could see only the top of the pin, which was perhaps 50 feet away. He blasted out of the sand, the ball bounced once and went into the cup for a birdie.

No such miracle shots occurred on the day in 1991 when George Bush, Reagan's Vice President who succeeded him in the Oval Office, invited Reagan for a game of golf during a brief visit to California. The two men were paired with another of Reagan's frequent golfing buddies, Arco chairman Lodwrick Cook, and longtime Bush backer Jerry Weintraub, a movie producer. They joshed with reporters and photographers on the first tee of the elegant Sherwood Country Club course in Thousand Oaks, near Los Angeles. Bush, then age 67, asked, "You got mulligans on this fancy course?"— before proving that he did, indeed, need a second shot. He duffed his first ball, then hit his mulligan well down the fairway.

Reagan, 11 years Bush's senior, apologized to the reporters about the quality of his game. "You might as well know my alibi in advance," he said. "I'm camera shy."

Thereupon, the former actor cracked his tee shot 150 yards down the left center of the fairway.

The result of that match—one of the rare meetings of two Presidents on the links—wasn't revealed, although the reporters said Bush seemed to have the upper hand. Yet no one could top Reagan when it came to dramatic flair. Two years earlier, as he prepared to leave the White House, the President met with the members of the Notre Dame football team, which had won the national championship that year. Since the day was unusually mild for January, the session took place in the Rose Garden, and Reagan was presented with the letter sweater that had belonged to George Gipp, whom he had portrayed in the movies. The President urged Notre Dame, this last time, to win one more "for the Gipper."

Observers said there wasn't a dry eye in the Rose Garden as Ronald Reagan walked into the twilight.

TERROR ON THE LINKS

While he was in the White House, Ronald Reagan scaled back significantly on his golf. That may have been just as well considering what occurred when he made his sole excursion to that great golfing mecca, the Augusta National Golf Club in Georgia. The visit produced a crisis of major proportions.

In the fall of 1983, Reagan was playing at Augusta with Senator Nicholas Brady of New Jersey against Secretary of State George

Shultz and Treasury Secretary Donald Regan. The foursome had reached the famous par-3 16th hole when word came that a terrorist had taken over the pro shop. An unemployed factory worker had crashed his pickup truck through one of the club's gates and, wielding a .35-caliber pistol, was holding seven people hostage, including two presidential aides—and was demanding to speak to the President.

Reagan was whisked into his armored limousine, from which he tried to reach the gunman by radio telephone, saying, "This is the President of the United States. I understand you want to talk to me." There were five or six such attempts, but the gunman remained silent, and Reagan's limo eventually roared away. Meanwhile, the pastoral Augusta setting began to take on all the trappings of an armed camp—with a storm of hovering helicopters, sheriff's deputies toting shotguns and Secret Service agents brandishing submachine guns. After a two-hour siege, during which the hostages were released one by one, the terrorist finally was taken into custody.

If that crisis was resolved, the status of the match was not. It seems Brady had put his tee shot at the 16th hole within gimme range before the President was taken away—meaning Reagan's twosome would have been three up with two holes to play, thereby winning the match. But in all the excitement, no one was ever paid.

CHAPTER 13

GEORGE BUSH
Golf in the Express Lane

The Secret Service agents who escorted him on the course referred to it facetiously as "power golf." Some of his frequent companions on the links named it "aerobic golf." Others knew it as "speed golf." He himself liked to call it "cart polo."

But by any name, the game of golf as played by George Bush was as frantic and fast-paced as a last-minute campaign swing. The object was simple: to complete a round quickly and in near-record time if possible. Bush and three others once flew around 18 holes in a supersonic one hour and 42 minutes. "We may not be good," the President hollered to a bemused foursome as he roared past them one Saturday, "but we're fast."

"We're not out there throwing grass up in the air, testing the winds," said son George W. Bush, the governor of Texas, who often played with his father. "We like to bang away. My father's measure of success is not how low you score, but how fast you play. His goal is to always finish 18 holes in less than three hours."

Golf exacts a price for every affront to convention, of course, and Bush paid for his pell-mell play with scores that weren't nearly as good as they might have been. "He plays so fast he doesn't have time to concentrate," said Ken Raynor, the professional at the Cape

Playing Through: Bush's goal was to play fast rather than score well. He and three others once raced around 18 holes in a supersonic 1 hour and 42 minutes. AP/WIDE WORLD PHOTOS

Arundel Golf Club, where Bush played while on holiday at his family's summer retreat in Kennebunkport, Maine. "There's definitely no deliberation over a shot," Raynor added. When he took his time and his game was cooking, the President had proved he could shoot as low as 76 at Cape Arundel, and, indeed, he won a tournament there as a young man. But when he played "cart polo," he generally produced scores in the upper 80s or low 90s while his handicap soared into the 20s when he was President.

Didn't his manic pace cost him when they tallied up the nassaus? Not a nickel. Wagering was as frowned on as taking time to beat the underbrush for a lost ball. "It's all done for respect—for bragging rights," said Raynor.

Why was Bush in such an all-fired rush?

"I play golf fast," he explained, "because I don't like to stand around and wait. Like a lot of other golfers, I get cold when I wait. Besides that, there are lots of other things to do. So get it on, play fast, go on to the next event." By nature, in fact, he was almost compulsively restless whether in the Oval Office, at a political wee- nie roast or on the fairway—so much so that around the White House during his one term from 1989 to 1993 they nicknamed him "the Mexican jumping bean." Few if any Presidents have had such itchy feet.

And none has been such a versatile athlete. Bush had an impec- cable, blue-blooded golfing pedigree as well as enough feel for the game to have boasted an 11 handicap in his younger days. But he played—and played with considerable skill—a number of other sports, too. So in addition to golf, he wanted to squeeze in time for jogging, for tennis, for fishing, for softball, for swim- ming, for horseshoes, for hunting and for boating. (On the water, nothing that could be as languid as sailing would do, of course; he raced around impetuously in Fidelity, his 28-foot, twin-engine cigarette boat.)

On some mornings when he was on holiday, he would announce to the media that he was undertaking a "quintathlon," which typi- cally might consist of a two-mile jog, two sets of tennis, a high- speed ride in Fidelity, 18 holes of golf and casting for striped bass in the Kennebunkport River. A *New York Times* editorial noted that "Mr. Bush works so hard at playing he may not notice the differ- ence when he returns to work" in the White House.

The Lessons of Golf

The President had more in mind than paring off a few pounds or escaping the tensions of his job when he played golf—or any sport, for that matter. "I'm a great believer that sports can do won- ders for friendships and establishing common ground," Bush said. "Have always felt that way. Still feel that way." Or as his son Marvin observed: "He thinks that competition, whether in the political arena or athletically, teaches you . . . that life isn't a straight shot north."

One lesson that golf taught the President, as well as everybody else who has ever succumbed to its bittersweet wiles, was, as he put

Graceful Moves: Bush had a
well-paced swing that generally
produced solid contact with the
ball. The best parts of his game were
his drives and his long iron shots.

it, "humiliation." He remarked glumly once that one of the local hazards at Cape Arundel "is being on the course when I play." Yet he did reasonably well at golf as President, considering that he never took a lesson, never practiced and, on those occasions in the summer when he could play, always circled a course in the express lane.

While Bush may not rank among the best or the most dedicated of White House golfers, he did play in the 1990 Doug Sanders Celebrity Classic, a Senior PGA Tour event in Kingswood, Texas. The description of the scene at Kingswood by David Casstevens of the *Dallas Morning News* gave a vivid indication of the perils a President faces when he takes his golf game public:

"Imagine trying to play golf surrounded by Secret Service agents, scores of them, their eyes hidden behind dark glasses anxiously searching the crowd. One carried a tan jacket under his arm [with] what appeared to be, judging by its shape, a large automatic weapon. It was no tennis racquet. You can bet on that. Imagine walking down a fairway with nine golf carts in tow. The sign on one read, 'Military Aide/Doctor.' In the back of [another] cart was a foldup stretcher. Imagine trying to play golf amid the crackle of walkie-talkies. Imagine standing over your ball on the tee box, preparing to swing . . . and someone in the huge gallery shouts, 'DOWN THE MIDDLE, MR. PRESIDENT!'"

Before Bush teed off that day, PGA commissioner Deane Beman presented him with an antique golf club. In accepting it, the President joked about his golfing inadequacies. "My wife, Barbara, wanted to be here," he said, "but she doesn't like to see her husband cry." And he made one request: "Please don't laugh at my drive off the first tee."

They didn't laugh. They ran for cover, because the first drive hooked left into the crowd. He then topped his second shot, but he drew sympathetic cheers from the crowd, anyway. "Everyone clapped for him," said one fan, "because that's the way most of us hit it." Once he got going, however, the President's game came together. He missed a six-foot putt for a birdie on the par-3 eighth hole and scored a heroic birdie on the 145-yard 12th by firing a 7-iron within four feet of the pin. "What's your handicap?" one spectator called out. "A lot," Bush replied as he hurried on.

He couldn't play at his customary breakneck pace, of course, under the tournament conditions. In fact, he had to wait for 10 minutes while Lee Trevino and his group teed off at the ninth hole. "Isn't this a great country?" Trevino quipped later. "Where else could a Mexican hold up the President of the United States?"

Strengths and Weaknesses

Bush was a natural left-hander who played golf right-handed (like Bobby Jones, among other famous golfers). "You can very much see the athlete in his swing," said Raynor. "It's well coordinated. The pace of the swing is one of his best attributes. He has a good grip, as well. His feet are a little wide at setup, and he doesn't transfer his weight the way he should. But he usually makes awfully good contact. . . . He can step up on the first tee, without any warm-up, and hit a good drive."

Which way did Bush's shots tend to go? "What day of the week is it?" Raynor responded. "He'll fade it one day, draw it the next. But in truth, his driving and long irons are the best parts of his game because he's strong and makes excellent contact. He's out-driven me." Since he could hit his long and middle irons with respectable accuracy, Bush could, as often as not, be near the green in regulation.

It was then that his game frequently went off the tracks. When he had a chip or bunker shot 30 feet from the pin, the ball was as likely to land in some distant oak grove as it was on the green.

"The President simply has no feel for distance and he doesn't know how to use his hands effectively," observed Max Elbin, the pro at the Burning Tree Club. "Concentrating on these shots is really tough for him. He likes to have a good time out there, so he'll be talking and joking while he's hitting. I know he wants to improve; he's told me so. But he just doesn't have the touch, or the seriousness to develop this finesse."

Believe it or not, it could get worse—once, that is, the President managed to get his ball on the green. Putting, at least during the early years of his administration, was his own personal Pearl Harbor. "I was four-putting regularly," he said later. "Nobody would give me an 18-inch putt. They'd just stand around and laugh. I jabbed the ball—I actually missed the ball one time—on the putting green. I would send the ball miles beyond the hole on a short putt. On a long putt, I'd put it about a third of the way to the hole. I was nervous, embarrassed. The worst part was that I knew I was going to miss. I had a fatal case of the yips."

A Thousand Putts of Light

The President experimented with every cure known to the peda-gogues of golf—putting left-handed, putting one-handed, putting cross-handed, everything. Finally, he grew so desperate that he took the extraordinary step of going public with the problem on national television. The President shared his anguish with the audience of the 1989 Kemper Open telecast and appealed for any

Anguish on the Green: The elongated Pole-Kat putter cured Bush's near fatal case of the yips — although he could still emote with the best of them when a putt missed. AP/WIDE WORLD PHOTOS

suggested remedies. Bush, who had used "a thousand points of light" as one of his campaign slogans, was soon overwhelmed with advice designed to achieve, as one writer put it, "a thousand putts of light."

In his search for a remedy, Bush had installed on the South Lawn of the White House grounds a 1,500-square-foot, nine-hole practice green that was made of artificial turf. (The $20,000 cost was covered by private donations.) "It was a good green," Bush said after he left office, and "you could control the speed of putts. . . . My wife, Barbara, and I used the putting green a fair amount, and we really enjoyed it."

But Bush didn't find a cure for his putting problems on that green. Instead, he found it when he began using the elongated, 48-inch Pole-Kat putter, the kind then gaining favor with older pros who were also tormented by the yips. Bush also obtained later a long putter made by T. P. Mills. Both, the experts said, helped him because, by making him stand more erectly over the ball, he had a better view of the line of the putt.

When Bush first used the Pole-Kat, Raynor reported, "he ran in a 20-footer and got a big smile on his face. He sank putts from all over the place for the rest of the day. He was delirious. He shot an 81, which is his best score in a long time. He came back out and played both Sunday and Monday. Suddenly, he enjoys playing golf again." (That unsolicited testimonial was found gold for the manufacturer of the long putter, and naturally it cashed in by trumpeting those words around the golf world.)

So the long putter immediately joined the other sticks in the President's red-and-black leather golf bag presented to him by the members of the 1991 U.S. Ryder Cup team when they visited the White House. The clubs included a Callaway "Big Bertha" driver given to him by Senator Sam Nunn of Georgia, a Democrat whose handicap of 6 made him one of the top golfers at the time among Washington dignitaries. "I can't hit the ball like he can," Bush admitted, "but I like the club." Also in his bag were a Callaway 7-wood, Arnold Palmer 3- and 5-woods, irons from Ray Floyd and three wedges with lofts of 48, 54 and 58 degrees. He used Titleist balls and special tees, both with his name on them.

Through the years, Bush played most of his golf during summers at the Cape Arundel course, just a five-minute drive from his family's 11-acre oceanfront compound in Kennebunkport. Cape Arundel is a links-style course, which Bush described as "a little tricky, a little water-infested [water and tidal flats come into play on 11 holes] but very nice. If you can hit the ball far, you have a real shot at birdies." During the winter, he would sometimes fly to Key Largo in Florida to golf at the Ocean Reef Club's two courses. Like his predecessor, Ronald Reagan, he broke one long-standing presidential tradition: He rarely golfed at the Burning Tree Club. He'd played there frequently during the eight years he was Vice President in Reagan's administration, but he backed off as President, apparently because the club refused to admit women— although he wouldn't confirm that was the reason.

Bush particularly enjoyed playing with his brothers and other family members. "We have a very competitive family," he said, "and that always [makes it] fun." Other favorite partners included such members of his administration as National Security Adviser Brent Scowcroft, Secretary of State James Baker, Transportation Secretary Samuel Skinner and Treasury Secretary Nicholas Brady, a low-handicapper and two-time champion at the Somerset Hills Country Club in Bernardsville, New Jersey. Bush golfed once with Ronald Reagan during his predecessor's retirement in California and didn't play much with his Vice President, Dan Quayle—but when he did, he said, "I enjoyed [it] because he's so darn good." (See the end of this chapter.)

A Presidential Performer

Bush claimed that he preferred privacy on the links. "A modest, kind of shy guy like me, I like to play golf without a lot of people watching," he said. "Once in a while, you take a practice putt and it doesn't go in, and then you see it on television. And then I have to explain to my grandchildren 'How come you missed it three times?' So you have these inhibitions."

Don't buy that line. Bush, according to Raynor at Cape Arundel, worked a golf course like a politician at a fund-raiser. "I guess it's the performer in him," Raynor remarked. "He'll shake hands with almost anybody who passes by. He passes out golf balls and tees with 'President' on them. He holds kids, signs scorecards and poses for photographs."

Whether playing before a crowd or in private with friends, Bush maintained a tireless bonhomie. He was as chatty as Trevino and as enthusiastic as any member of a public course dawn patrol. "All right," he would say cheerily as his foursome gathered on a first tee. "It's dog-eat-dog. No favors. No friends." He underscored the point once by planting an exploding chalk ball on the tee of Scowcroft. When Scowcroft swung lustily at the ball, it disintegrated into a cloud of white dust—leaving Bush in stitches and the shaken White House aide lamenting, "I should have known that ball looked funny."

As a round progressed, Bush would punctuate it with a stream of quips. For instance, when playing with his sons one day, he said he was dedicating a particular chip shot to his wife, "who's been such a wonderful father to these boys here." He asked for gimme putts by intoning solemnly, "In respect for my high office, isn't that putt good?" He also liked to portray himself in dramatic situations. "Here we are on the 18th at Pebble Beach," he would declare. "Let me show you how it's done." He not only talked to his companions, he talked to his ball. "C'mon, left," he would urge it. "I want to get near the green." Or, "Oh, golly darn, get up there."

He even had his own on-course patois. He mockingly identified himself as Mr. Smooth. A colleague who was playing badly was called Arnold Farmer. A weak shot was "a power outage." A sand trap was "wedge city." And victory was "Vic Damone." (When word of that last expression reached singer Damone, he phoned the President to tell him that "when I sink a long putt, I am now yelling 'George Bush!'")

Bush was, in short, the most engaging of companions out on a course. Golf writer and novelist Dan Jenkins played 18 holes with Bush and reported in *Golf Digest*: "If it's a fact that a man reveals his true character on a golf course, I can only attest that the President was easier to be around than any captain of industry I've ever been paired with in a pro-am. . . . He was the friendliest and most relaxed person . . . on every fairway."

Bush, characteristically, had problems with his pitches and chips on the first three holes, Jenkins said, "mainly because he was rushing his swing. He plays fast, I am happy to report, and doesn't understand why anybody would play slowly. He could do mankind a wonderful service, I suggested, if he signed into law the death penalty for slow-playing golfers."

The President got his game more in sync on the back nine. At the 145-yard 12th hole, a par 3, he hit an iron shot that parked the ball on the front of the green 12 feet from the pin. After he putted out for a par, one member of the gallery hollered: "How do you like the course, Mr. President?"

"Great!"

"How's your game?"

"Yeah!"

Bush's Grandfather: George Herbert Walker (right) was head of the U.S. Golf Association when he presented the 1920 National Amateur Championship trophy to Chick Evans. UPI/BETTMANN

Great Golfing Genes

If anyone was ever born with a silver spoon in his golf bag, it was George Herbert Walker Bush. Consider these legacies.

His maternal grandfather, George Herbert Walker, was president of the U.S. Golf Association in 1920. Upon leaving office, he established the Walker Cup, the trophy given ever since to the winning team in the biennial competition between top U.S. and British amateur golfers. It may have been from Walker that his grandson got an itch for speedy golf. Said one family friend: "The Walkers used to play fast, too."

The President's father, Prescott Bush, also served as a president of the USGA (in 1935) before becoming a U.S. senator from

Connecticut. The senator, a superb golfer, was an eight-time club champion at the Cape Arundel Golf Club in Kennebunkport. He held the course record of 66 there for years.

The President's earliest golfing memories, he said, involved going with his mother and brothers to watch his father "as he came up the 18th hole of some tournament or other. Then, as youngsters, we'd sit around and hear [my uncles] talking about how Dad had beat them up on the golf course. He was good." So good that when he played in his first National Seniors tournament, he shot a first-round 66 and a 71 the next day to finish second.

How did such feats affect his son when he took up the game as a boy. "It affected me by being a little bit intimidating," the President conceded. "I've never liked to do anything poorly, so I think Dad's scratch handicap inspired me in some ways and intimidated me in others. . . . I guess I was like any other kid. You start swinging away like mad and every once in a while make contact. I never learned under the leadership of a teacher."

The President stayed with the game through his adolescent and college years. At Yale, he was good enough to captain a baseball team that twice made it to the NCAA championship final. But, he said, "I was clearly not golf team material, although I had a lot of fun" at the game. In fact, he golfed enough during this period at the "monster" Yale course, at a nearby municipal layout in New Haven, Connecticut, and at Kennebunkport to become sufficiently good to win a Cape Arundel tournament.

After graduation from Yale, Bush headed for the oil business in Midland, Texas, and for a lot of frenzied weekend golf during the next dozen years. The winds howling in off the west Texas prairies at the Midland Country Club made the game something of a challenge. But Bush was usually equal to it. It was there that he achieved the one golf feat he would most often mention in later years: an eagle on a par-4 hole, using his 5-iron for the second shot. And it was there that his handicap topped out at a career-best 11, a pinnacle from which it beat a dismaying retreat once he left Texas for a succession of big jobs in government that led to the White House.

As President, Bush made no attempt to hide his golfing side as some of his predecessors had done. In fact, he almost flaunted it. He whizzed President Mikhail Gorbachev of the Soviet Union around Camp David in a golf cart as photographers and TV camera crews recorded the ride. One time in Bermuda, moreover, the President interrupted a major conference with Prime Minister Margaret Thatcher of Great Britain to work in a round of golf with her husband, Denis—although who knows why they bothered. It was raining, and the wind was blowing so intensely that small-craft warnings were flying and palm trees were blown inside out like crippled umbrellas. That didn't daunt an intrepid Bush, who had a cold at the time. "It refurbishes the spirit," he called out to reporters as he half-sprinted down the first fairway into the soaking rain and wind.

The Golf Crisis

It's possible, however, to overdo such grittiness. And some thought the President did that in the summer of 1990 after he put the country on a war footing with Iraq. He was resolved to avoid any appearance that he was imprisoned in the White House by Saddam Hussein's military threats in the Persian Gulf as Jimmy Carter had been a decade earlier by the hostage crisis in Iran. "I'm determined that life goes on," he said.

So he spent his August holiday in Kennebunkport grimly pursuing all of his usual sporting interests. His golf, though, was the one that got top billing. It was cited in many media reports about the build-up in the Gulf. He issued some statements from the first tee at Cape Arundel. He was photographed using the emergency mobile phone in his golf cart.

That kind of thing didn't play too well in many quarters. Critics jumped on the President for golfing while the U.S. troops he'd sent to the Persian Gulf were facing a war. Others had fun with the situation. The Gulf crisis, perhaps inevitably, was christened the "golf crisis" by headline writers. By the time the real shooting started in

A Menacing Ayatollah: An editorial cartoon depicted the pressure Iran was putting on Bush in 1989. NEW YORK POST CARTOON BY BAY RIGBY. REPRINTED WITH PERMISSION, THE NEW YORK POST

the Gulf, though, Bush was back in the White House, far from the links and safe from the summer's golf barbs.

While Bush won accolades internationally for his handling of the Gulf War, he didn't fare so well afterward on the domestic golfing front. Indeed, he found a sterner adversary than Saddam Hussein in one individual: his wife. Barbara Bush had, at the President's suggestion, resumed golf after 20 years so that they could play together at Kennebunkport. But when they tried, it was a disaster—as Franklin and Eleanor Roosevelt had found years earlier (see chapter 6).

The President told reporters bluntly that his wife's game "stunk." That was a fighting word. For when Mrs. Bush was told of the remark and was asked if she would golf with her husband in the future, she snapped, "Never again."

The next summer, as he began his reelection campaign of 1992, Bush was seldom seen playing with anyone. The criticism he'd gotten for golfing during the Gulf crisis was still fresh in his advisers' minds.

But when he lost the election anyway, Bush returned promptly to the links. Within three weeks, he was back in Kennebunkport for some well-publicized golf and some Thanksgiving turkey. As a headline in the *New York Daily News* put it: "Bush Slices Ball Before Carving Bird." Then, as he settled into retirement, his wife relented and agreed to play golf with him. "I can't give him any competition," Mrs. Bush conceded, "but I am the only one who will play at 6:00 A.M. with 10 minutes notice."

Improvement, At Last

Bush discovered that there were definite drawbacks in leaving the White House. "For one thing," he quipped in a Dallas speech, "I find that I no longer win every golf game I play." Nonetheless, he did begin to play better. It wasn't that he finally slowed his pace of play. The improvement came, in part, because he began practicing for the first time in years and, in part, because the immense stresses of the presidency had been lifted from him.

Cape Arundel pro Raynor said that Bush had, for one thing, at last mastered the "short little chip shot—a shot that takes delicacy and finesse. He used to have a lot of tension in his hands. You need to be relaxed to do this shot, and now he's relaxing more on the golf course."

But he didn't all the time—most notably when he found himself during 1993, as he had three years earlier, in the daunting company of some big-name pros at the Doug Sanders Celebrity Classic in Kingwood, Texas. "On the practice tee," as Bush told it, "I somehow managed to hit one right off the end of the club. . . . It kind of rolled down the shaft and hit Dan Quayle on the top of the head." Then, on the first tee, his drive skimmed over spectators' heads and sailed into the woods. He then hit a second drive, and that one whacked a spectator on the leg. Said Bush of the experience, "I doubt that I'll do many celebrity tournaments in the future."

Still, such misadventures didn't dismay an exuberant golfer like Bush for long. "It only takes a few good holes to make you want to come back," he said. If he played a bad round or two, he added, he would still "have this feeling that tomorrow it's going to be fine. Tomorrow I'll be doing well.

"That's golf."

DAN QUAYLE'S GAME: "100 PERCENT SILK"

Dan Quayle, the Vice President in the Bush administration, was beyond question the best golfer that the country had yet elected on a national ticket. Among his many exploits, Quayle:

- Won the congressional golfing championship while a senator from Indiana and twice captured his club title at the Fort Wayne Country Club.
- Defeated his pro partner, Joey Sindelar, by four strokes at a Kemper Open. Sindelar, at the time, ranked 16th on the pro tour's prize-money list for the year.
- Came close to matching the drive of the megahitting pro, John Daly, on the 18th hole at a Bob Hope Desert Classic. Quayle's ball soared 273 yards, only about 20 yards short of Daly's drive.
- Carded a 73 on his initial round at a course in Port Douglas, Australia, to beat the club's house pro, who had a 75.

Quayle had to make something of a golfing sacrifice after he became Vice President. Bowing to the demands of his new job as well as the possibility of criticism from Democrats, he limited himself to one or two rounds a week in season, which for him represented a cruel cutback from the three or four weekly rounds he had enjoyed while serving in Congress. His handicap, consequently, rose from three to seven.

Bush and Quayle (right):
Playing to a handicap as low as
three, the Vice President was
the best golfer yet elected
on a national ticket.
AP/WIDE WORLD PHOTOS

Still, he maintained the basic elements of a game that was, marveled one reporter, "100 percent silk." He combined a sublime natural swing with a lifetime of golfing experience and an abiding fervor for the game. "Dan Quayle would rather play golf than have sex any day," according to a reliable source—his wife, Marilyn.

Quayle possessed a swing that could drive the ball into the next area code. He used a slightly narrow, slightly open stance, a neutral grip and a simple, compact swing that was even in tempo. He meshed right-to-left power with a keen strategic sense. "He knows when to be aggressive and when to back off," said Bill Kratzert, head pro at the Fort Wayne club.

Like Bush, Quayle had the kind of strong family roots in golf that delight traditionalists. Both of the Vice President's grandfathers had been formidable golfers. Robert H. Quayle had been a scratch player, while the Vice President's maternal grandfather, press lord Eugene Pulliam, once shot a 62 in the Florida state amateur tournament.

One of Dan Quayle's earliest golf experiences came as a boy when he tagged along while Pulliam played a round with President Dwight D. Eisenhower. And when Quayle took up the game himself at age 10, he climbed the junior golf ladder like Arnold Palmer in his prime moving up a fourth-round leader board. By the time he was 12, Quayle had won his first tournament with a round of 82. By 15 his bedroom was crowded with golf trophies. By 17 he had his first hole-in-one. By 18 he had shot a 68 and lowered his handicap to four. By graduation from DePauw University in Green-castle, Indiana, he had played number one on a collegiate golf team that never lost.

"I tell you, that boy was one hell of a golfer," said DePauw golf coach Ted Katula. "I mean, he could hit. Drives in the high 200s, low 300s, right around there. He played by the seat of his pants. Danny had no fear at all. He'd just step up and fire." Katula thought that, with work, the talent was there for the pro tour.

Quayle doubted that. "I was lucky," he said. "I wasn't good enough to give it serious thought."

CHAPTER 14

BILL CLINTON
The Happy Golfer

S hortly before Bill Clinton decided to make his run for the presidency in 1992, he was playing golf with Senator David Pryor of Arkansas one afternoon in Little Rock. Nothing had been said about the presidential race through the first 17 holes. Then, on the 18th, Clinton sliced his drive into the rough behind a pine tree.

As he surveyed the situation, Clinton turned to Pryor and asked, "What should I do?"

The senator suggested using a 2-iron to hit the ball back onto the fairway.

"No," Clinton replied. "What I want to know is, should I run for President?"

It didn't seem to require much persuasion to convince him to enter the race. And when he won the White House, Clinton brought with him a zest for golf that has placed him among the most fervent of presidential players, although not among the best of them. Talk about fervent: On his first full day of vacation in 1995, Clinton got in fully 37 holes of golf at Jackson Hole, Wyoming. There were two complete rounds of 18 holes, but that wasn't enough. He then had to play one extra hole for good measure. No

The Joy of Golf: Clinton (here with golf buddy Vernon Jordan) plays at country clubs, but, says one observer, "has the soul of a public-links player." REUTERS/BETTMANN

wonder *Golf Digest* named him its "Man of the Year" for 1995. He even enjoys the inevitable bad rounds. "The great thing about this game," Clinton once remarked, "is that the bad days are wonderful."

The attitude is contagious. "He is probably more sheer fun than anyone I've ever played with—and that's thousands of people," says Roy Neel, president of the U.S. Telephone Association. "He has a real appreciation [of golf], but he's not a purist." That's for sure. Clinton has aggravated some with his leisurely pace of play, stretched the rules with his use of mulligans and offended some dress codes with his scruffy attire when golfing out of public view. He also likes to chomp on a golf tee or an unlit cigar while on the course. One writer has described the first President to have been a Rhodes Scholar this way: "He might play at country clubs, but he has the soul of a public-links player."

Clinton, whom some in the media have dubbed the First Golfer, is invariably the self-appointed member of a foursome in charge of seeing that everyone is enjoying himself. He's out there constantly chatting, telling jokes, patting backs, offering congratulations on good shots and condolences on poor ones, talking about golf equipment, yelling at his ball, philosophizing about playing conditions and seeking advice from better players. "He made everyone else comfortable," said real-estate developer Charles Farish after a round with Clinton at the Sandpiper Golf Course in Santa Barbara, California. "He looked for everyone's golf balls. He was just a golfer. After nine holes, he said, 'What can I get you guys to drink?' I thought, 'Damn! The President of the United States!'"

But Clinton is also ready with a zinger now and then, such as the one he aimed at Sheldon Hackney, chairman of the National Endowment for the Humanities. After Hackney hit several wild drives, the President told him, "I've got a new idea. Try the fairway!"

A Perfect Fit

The joviality is, in part, an effort to help partners relax, because Clinton recognizes that playing with a President can be a daunting experience. "I was so nervous I went from sand trap to sand trap," confesses Jeremy Orchin, the orthodontist for Clinton's daughter, Chelsea. But mostly the levity is a reflection of the fact that golf seems to be a perfect fit for the Clinton persona. "It's hard to imagine Clinton skiing," observed Ruth Marcus of *The Washington Post*. "Who would he talk to on the way down?"

All the banter consumes a fair amount of time, of course. That, combined with his slow, deliberate style of play, means that a typical Clinton round can take five or more hours to complete. It annoys some, but Clinton will have it no other way. "What I like about golf is what other people dislike—it takes so long to play," he says. "I like the time it takes. Sometimes it takes me five or six holes to get into the game." There's no telling how long his rounds would last if the President were a gambling man who, like Warren G. Harding, paused to make numerous bets along the way. But the most Clinton will wager is the price of a round of Cokes or beers afterward in the clubhouse.

Only one topic is taboo during a Clinton match—politics. If anyone brings the subject up, the President will quickly steer the conversation back to golf. There have been, however, the rare exceptions. Little Rock attorney Mark Grobmyer can remember only one of them during his 20 years of golfing with the President. That was the weekend before Clinton settled on Albert Gore as his vice presidential running mate in 1992. "He talked a lot about that," says Grobmyer (who, in fact, introduced Clinton and Gore to each other in 1987). "That's about the only serious thing we've ever talked about" while on the links.

Airmailing the Ball

Amid the chitchat, Clinton can play a passable game. The President "is a good athlete," says Steve Tobash, the pro at the Army-Navy Country Club in Arlington, Virginia, where Clinton frequently golfs when he is in Washington. "He hits a lot of good shots. He has a good swing, and he's in balance. If you have a good swing, all the other parts of the game will come around." The President has a disconcerting habit of rising to the top of his left toe—and bending his left knee forward instead of to the right—at the top of his backswing. And his "flying" right elbow, coupled with a rapid swing, has led to a certain amount of inconsistency. Clinton generally hits the ball with a slight fade, moving it across the fairway from left to right, but when he connects off the tee, he can airmail the ball. His longest drives, according to Tobash, soar 275 yards or so. (He outdrove Jack Nicklaus twice during a round they played in Vail, Colorado.)

The President can also be deft with his Ping irons. Indeed, his proudest golfing moment to date came during a round in Little Rock when his drive put the ball on a root under a low-hanging tree. Clinton took his 3-iron and punched the ball, which then ran

*On Bended Knee: Clinton's
inconsistency stems from
the way he rises on his toe to
bend his left knee and lets his
right elbow fly from his side.
He also swings too rapidly.*
© 1995 NYT SPORTS/LEISURE
MAGAZINES

160 yards straight into the cup for an eagle. "He was jumping up and down, telling everybody about it, just like any golfer," recalls one of his partners. Clinton has less luck in sand traps, a major shortcoming in his game. Otherwise, his short game is adequate, although he does have a tendency to chili dip or flub the ball badly on chip shots. And since he is calm and confident on the greens, putting is a fairly reliable part of his game.

So what does all this add up to on the presidential scorecard? The answer is clouded by the matter of mulligans, which he uses freely—if not as brazenly as Lyndon B. Johnson. Clinton admits to one mulligan per round. But others put the number higher. It is said, for instance, that with friends in Little Rock the standard arrangement was one extra tee shot and two extra fairway shots per nine holes.

But orthodontist Orchin reports that during his round with the President "we played legitimate golf," other than taking mulligans on the first hole—"which is the American thing to do." Clinton is also defended by Tim Spring, the pro at the Mink Meadows Golf Club on Martha's Vineyard, Massachusetts, where the Clintons have vacationed. When he and the President played, Spring says, Clinton "tried to play his original golf ball. . . . If he hits a second, he will go back to the original ball. He usually does take one mulligan per 18 holes, like most."

The issue has even prompted *The New Yorker* to take an editorial stand. Part of a President's job, its writer noted, is "to set an example for the American electorate and the entire free world. . . . What worries me about Clinton is that the other day, after finishing the round in which he'd taken his first drive over, he bragged about shooting an 82, and seemed to genuinely believe that he was only three strokes away from his grand, self-proclaimed goal of breaking into the 70s."

Some friends say that the use of mulligans in Clinton foursomes reflects his "generous spirit." Others suggest it is part of his effort to help partners relax and enjoy themselves. It certainly contributes to the slow pace of a Clinton round.

The mulligan stew thus makes it difficult to get a precise handle on Clinton's handicap. It is usually said to be in the 12 to 18 range. The most reliable figure, however, probably comes from his home course at the Chenal Country Club in Little Rock. There he is considered a 20-handicapper.

A Presidential Milestone

There were, however, no mulligans requested or granted during the most publicized match in the history of presidential golf. That was the February 1995 meeting in Indian Wells, California, of Clinton and two of his predecessors: Gerald R. Ford and George Bush. It was the first time that three U.S. Presidents had played golf together. Their match was staged as part of the Bob Hope Chrysler Classic pro-am event. The details were featured the next day on front pages across the country, and taped highlights of the match were shown for the better part of an hour on NBC-TV.

The three Presidents played in a fivesome with Hope and Scott Hoch, the tournament's defending champion. Other pro-am groups included such golf icons as Arnold Palmer, Tom Kite and Curtis Strange and such celebrities as Clint Eastwood and Johnny Bench.

Clinton admitted to butterflies beforehand—as did his presidential partners. "We are nervous as cats," Clinton told the media. The stress showed when he spent more than an hour on the practice range; normally, he disdains that ritual and impatiently heads straight for the first tee. Bush remarked before he teed off that his goal was "just to get the ball in the air." Said Ford: "I would advise people they should stay behind us"—which proved to be a prescient warning after he and Bush proceeded to hit three spectators (see chapter 1).

Ford and Bush played to 18-handicaps while Clinton was put down for an 11. Strange, who had played a round with Clinton at Williamsburg, Virginia, rolled his eyes when he heard that latter figure. As the round progressed, the presidential trio joshed each other about the wounded spectators, praised each other's drives, sympathized with each other's poor shots and awarded each other gimme putts. But there were subtle signs of intramural competition and a slight chill between Bush and Clinton in the aftermath of their intense 1992 battle for the White House.

Bush provided the highlight of the round when he drained a 20-foot chip shot for a birdie at the 15th hole. But that was it for great shots. Indeed, on the next hole, Bush's drive sailed into the gallery; it didn't nail anyone, but he took a double bogey.

None of the Presidents scored well. After the five-and-one-half-hour match ended, Bush was credited officially with a 93, Clinton with a 95 and Ford with a 103. Afterward, NBC analyst and former U.S. Open champion Johnny Miller critiqued Clinton's game. He lacked consistency, Miller observed, but he could help correct that "if he could position his right elbow closer to his right hip at the top of his backswing. [He should] then physically place his elbow on that hip halfway down. It would make all the difference in the world."

Up from the Caddie Shack

Clinton started out in the game in the most time-honored way—as a caddie. At 12, he began caddieing and playing a bit at a course in Hot Springs, Arkansas. He had an early brush with championship-caliber golf when he carried for a group that included pro star Tommy "Thunder" Bolt, who played in a tournament in Hot Springs during the early 1960s. But Clinton gave up golf temporarily about the time he got his first driver's license at 16.

He likes to say that he was no jock in school, that he was "the fat kid in the band." But he was a decent enough athlete. He played church league basketball and, at Oxford as a Rhodes Scholar, was on the B basketball team. He also absorbed some hammering at Oxford on the rugby field. "I played one game with a minor concussion because there was no substitution," Clinton recalls. "You can get your head kicked in pretty easily, but I loved rugby. It was a good, rough game." (Much later, in a less violent form of competition, he could go down to the bowling alley in the White House basement and sometimes roll a game as high as 220.)

After he completed Yale Law School in 1973, Clinton returned to Arkansas and soon picked up his clubs again. Later, as governor of the state for 12 years, he would generally play twice a month, sometimes even in wintry weather. As President, he has actually increased his rounds to at least one a week. When he can, Clinton will grab his clubs at the end of the day and take off for a nearby course with Deputy Chief of Staff Erskine Bowles. That amount of play makes good sense to Robert Armstrong, a longtime golfing partner of Clinton's and an Interior Department official. "Golf is more important when you don't have time to play it," Armstrong says, pointing out it's then that the player most needs a break.

Sometimes, though, small matters can go as wrong for a President as they can for anybody else. For instance, Clinton was playing one day in Bismarck, North Dakota, with two Democratic senators, Byron Dorgan of North Dakota and Charles Robb of Virginia. At the third hole, nature called for the President. But the nearest rest room ahead of them was four holes away. So Robb rode to the rescue by driving his cart over to a woman who was standing outside her home beside the fairway and asking her if the President could use her bathroom. He did, and as they drove away, the golf party could hear her exclaiming, "God, this is a great country. Can you believe it? The President of the United States uses our bathroom and, Ernie, you didn't even vote for him!"

Golf on the Grounds

Clinton has followed Dwight D. Eisenhower's example by arranging things so that he can practice golf shots without leaving the White House grounds. Like Ike, he practices shots on the South Lawn. He is particularly proud of a monster drive that nearly cleared a White House fence 300 yards away. And Ike's putting green, which had been plowed under during the administration of Richard M. Nixon, has been restored outside the Oval Office. The cost, as it was with George Bush's White House green, was met by

Reading the Green: Clinton is considered a reliable putter even though the old, beat-up model he uses is, he said, "something like you'd find at an aging miniature golf course."

private donations. Bush's artificial turf was taken up and the new grass was planted atop the base of Ike's old green, which was found still intact. The restored green has five holes, each with a flagstick bearing the presidential seal. One hole is in the center with the four others placed around the perimeter.

Clinton uses the green four or five times a week when conditions outside permit. "It's a think tank," says White House aide George Stephanopoulos. "It's quiet, there are no phones, and he can use the game to distract part of his mind and let the other part do its work." Sometimes, others join him. On a summer afternoon, for example, the members of the National Security Council followed him out to the putting green to finish a discussion on the crisis in Bosnia. Occasionally, Clinton and Bowles move back 60 yards or so and from there play to the green as if it's a regular hole on a course—minus the first one or two shots.

The green is completely screened from public view. The easiest way to determine its position is to examine the back of a $20 bill, which depicts the White House. Starting with the 20 in the lower left-hand corner, move up and to the right of the zero. That's the green's location.

On the course, Clinton is by far the most casually dressed of all the presidential golfers. For games with his cronies, he has been known to turn up outfitted in sweatshirts and chinos, or sports shirts and wheat-jean cutoffs, or jogging suits. He frequently wears running shoes rather than golf shoes. One day he sported a long-sleeved burgundy T-shirt with this enigmatic inscription: "Bryn Mawr College Physics Department (1895–1994). One Hundred and Nine Years of Women in Classically Forbidden Regions." *Sports Illustrated* was appalled by Clinton's wardrobe during a round right after the 1992 election. "He wore jogging shoes, and his shirt was hanging out over painter's pants," the magazine reported. "Golf needs Clinton like it needs a case of ringworm."

The President's attire is equally informal when he goes jogging, his main form of exercise. He welcomes companions, largely, it would seem, because it gives him people to talk and joke with along the way. There are so many politicians, officials and others who ask to join him that one White House official says, "Jogging with the President is bigger than an audience in the Oval Office." One object of the jogging is to keep him in good shape for golf. In fact, it may be a principal reason he is able to get stronger as a round progresses and is particularly solid on the back nine.

Where He Plays

Saturdays when he's in Washington, Clinton usually tackles Arlington's Army-Navy Country Club course with three companions he brings along with him. As Ronald Reagan and Bush had done, he spurns the club that has been most associated with presidential golf since the Eisenhower years. The Burning Tree Club in Bethesda, Maryland, is a men-only facility, and that is apparently a reason Reagan, Bush (while President) and Clinton have ignored it— although none of them has said so.

During his presidential campaign, moreover, Clinton had learned about the commotion that can be created when a politician frequents a club that discriminates. He had been playing occasionally as a guest at the Country Club of Little Rock, an all-white club that was organized in 1902 and is, therefore, one of the oldest clubs west of the Mississippi. When his attendance at the club was revealed, there was a torrent of criticism, and Clinton promptly admitted he had made a mistake. He would never play there again, he announced, until blacks were admitted as members.

Following the 1992 election, Clinton concentrated on setting up his new administration while also working in some golf at the Chenal Club (women and blacks admitted) in Little Rock. Nothing interfered with his Saturday morning rounds, not even raw weather with temperatures in the 30s. On one occasion, rain had created a puddle on a green between Clinton's ball and the hole. He was putting for a birdie. But the puddle slowed the putt, and it missed the hole by a few inches. He joked, "I tried to get the guys I played with to give me an eight-inch water allowance." On another dreary day, he lost two balls in the fog.

Clinton also got an early introduction to the invasion of privacy a presidential golfer has to suffer, and he didn't suffer it gladly. When he showed up at the Chenal Club on the first weekend after the 1992 election, for example, he discovered several news photographers at the first tee. Angered and cursing briefly, he complained loudly to the club manager, "I thought we had an agreement that they weren't going to be up here." He cooled down quickly and learned he would have to live with such intrusions.

That Christmas, Hillary Rodham Clinton gave her husband a set of Ping Eye2 irons to go with his Callaway Big Bertha driver and a vintage Bulls Eye putter. He actually misplaced the putter just before his match with Bush and Ford, but it didn't seem like much of a loss from the way he described it. "It's at least 35 years old and beat up," he said. "Something like you'd find at an aging miniature golf course." He also received a new golf bag for Christmas, but he refused to use it until he was in the White House because it had the presidential seal on the side. (He subsequently ordered four pairs of Foot-Joy golf shoes with the presidential seal on them.)

Favorite Partners

As President, Clinton delights in playing with a wide variety of golfers. (All partners receive a White House golf ball.) Among the rich and famous are such show business figures as actor James Garner, businessmen such as Microsoft founder William Gates Jr. and investment wizard Warren Buffett, as well as the biggest name of all in golf: Jack Nicklaus. The Nicklaus match, Clinton said, "reminds me of a decision I made, at an earlier stage of my life, not to become a professional musician. I played [the tenor saxophone] with someone who was really great, and I looked at that guy and said, 'I'll never be that good. I better find another line of work.'"

A favorite Clinton partner is Vernon E. Jordan, a Washington lawyer/lobbyist who was the President's transition chief. He acted as the Clintons' unofficial host when they spent summer vacations on Martha's Vineyard. According to some cynics, Jordan fills the

Daunting Opponent: Clinton delights in playing with such notables as Jack Nicklaus (left) and Gerald R. Ford. Watching Nicklaus play, he said, reminded him of his decision not to be a professional musician: "I'll never be that good. I better find another line of work." AP/WIDE WORLD PHOTOS

important role of making the President's average golf game look good by comparison.

Clinton also continues to arrange games with his golfing buddies from Arkansas. The most prominent of those used to be Webster L. Hubbell, who was a partner of Hillary Clinton's in the Rose Law Firm in Little Rock and who served as the number-three official in Clinton's Department of Justice. "Golf is an escape for Bill," said Hubbell, who golfed with him for more than 20 years. "He'll call and say, 'I can get away. Can you?' It's a chance to laugh and tell stories. For the first few holes, he's just warming up. Then he'll get around the turn and really start bearing down on you. A real good athlete. A real good attitude." Scandal, however, brought a quick end to Hubbell's government service in 1994 when he admitted to tax evasion and mail fraud while he had been at the Rose firm. (He began serving a 21-month prison term in the summer of 1995.)

A few weeks after Hubbell's disgrace, a golf scandal broke inside the White House. Its director of administration, David Watkins, had commandeered a presidential helicopter and used it with two aides to fly to Camp David and then to the Holly Hills Country Club in Maryland for an afternoon of golf. Watkins's excuse was that he and his party were scouting out the course as a possible place for the President to play. A furious Clinton wouldn't have any of that. When he learned of the boondoggle, he sacked Watkins immediately and ordered him to reimburse the government for the $13,129.66 that the trip had cost.

There have been times when Clinton has used golf for political ends—such as the occasions when he offered to play golf with several congressmen if they would vote for his economic package in 1993 and the North American Free Trade Agreement in 1994.

But his golf was turned against him during a budget crisis late in 1995. One Saturday, Clinton denounced his Republican opponents in Congress as "deeply irresponsible." He then went off to play golf. When the Republicans heard about that, Senate Majority Leader Bob Dole and House Speaker Newt Gingrich showed up in the Senate press gallery—with Gingrich wielding a golf club. They then chastised the President in sometimes sarcastic terms for placing his golf game ahead of solving the budget impasse.

A Tip from Tom Watson

A Clinton policy also managed to upset some of the top U.S. professional golfers. It was the tax increases imposed on the wealthy in 1993 by his administration and Congress. The group of pros reportedly included Payne Stewart, Corey Pavin and Lee Janzen. In fact, it was said that some members of the 1993 U.S. Ryder Cup team were so angered by the increases that they wanted to boycott a private White House reception for the team before it left to take on a European squad in England. But none did. Team captain Tom Watson maintained that the matter "was really blown out of proportion." He did concede, however, that "some of the players came to me and apologized that this thing got out in the first place."

A Lesson in the Rose Garden: While some Ryder Cup team members griped about Clinton's tax policies, 1993 captain Tom Watson (left) rounded them all up and even gave the President a pointer on his grip. Looking on: team members Chip Beck, John Cook, Raymond Floyd and Lee Janzen (far right). AP/WIDE WORLD PHOTOS

The reception in the Rose Garden turned out to be a big success, and Clinton even got a pointer from Watson on how to grip a club. "I tried to impress upon the President that if you grip the club with too strong a left hand, the ball goes left," Watson said. "If you use too strong a right hand, it goes right. The trick is to find a grip that hits it down the middle. When I told him that, the President laughed and said he tries to do that with everything, not just golf."

As the 30-minute visit ended, Clinton seemed reluctant to let the golfers go. Team member Paul Azinger reported that Clinton "said this was typical of being President. As soon as you start having some fun, they make you do something else." His final words to the Cup team were, "Bring it back." The players obliged, beating the Europeans 15 to 13.

Clinton obviously relishes moments like that one, when he can mix with famed touring pros or play with some of them. How much do those occasions mean to him? That was revealed later when he put it all in perspective as only a genuine golf fanatic can. "Of all the perks that come with being President of the United States," Clinton said, "the best one is being able to play 18 holes of golf with Arnold Palmer."

HILLARY RODHAM CLINTON: AN UNDERSTANDING GOLF WIDOW

"All I know is that for the first time in our married life, Hillary told me I had to play golf this morning," said Bill Clinton. "That was the first indication I had that something funny was going on."

What was going on was perhaps the most inventive birthday present a First Lady has given to a golfing President. For his 49th birthday, Hillary Rodham Clinton surprised her husband by arranging a round of golf for him with Johnny Miller, the onetime professional star and current TV golf commentator. They played in August 1995 at the Jackson Hole Golf & Tennis Club in Wyoming where the Clintons were vacationing. Clinton shot an 89 while Miller had a 69.

Hillary Clinton, like many First Ladies before her, is no grieving golf widow. She recognizes therapeutic benefits of the game for someone shouldering the burdens of the presidency. And although she was an avid athlete in her younger years, she has rarely attempted golf. Not that she hasn't received an earful about it from her husband after his rounds. "I get a full report on every . . . single . . . hole," she has said. "I mean it's just a part of the ritual. He'll come

Body English: Hillary Rodham Clinton coaxed a putt toward the hole during a 1994 summer vacation on Martha's Vineyard in Massachusetts. AP/WIDE WORLD PHOTOS

in and start in [she makes her voice deeper]: 'There we were on the fourth hole and so-and-so hit this long drive . . . .'"

She has taken golf lessons three times but hasn't cared for the game. The President tried to change that during their summer vacation in 1994 on Martha's Vineyard in Massachusetts. She had done a little putting as a lark. So he persuaded her to join him for nine holes at the Mink Meadows Golf Club.

His timing, though, could hardly have been worse. A driving rain and high winds were battering the course—so much so that the Clintons would be the only players out there. The First Lady gamely agreed to play and did about as well as any golf novice could under the conditions. On her first attempt to tee off, the club ripped up a tuft of sod. The second try produced a ball that popped straight up in the air. The third shot went 75 yards right down the fairway.

The President, hoping she would persevere in golf, remarked that "the trick for all beginners is not to be impatient. You have to keep at it, you know—sort of like life."

CHAPTER 15

HOOVER, TRUMAN AND CARTER

The Three Renegades

Of all the U.S. Presidents elected since William Howard Taft introduced golf to the White House, only three have bought into Mark Twain's dour dictum that "golf is a good walk spoiled" and spurned the sport completely. The heretics: Herbert Hoover, Harry Truman and Jimmy Carter.

Each had an excuse—sort of. Hoover was too much of a workaholic to spare the time, Truman never demonstrated a talent or an inclination for any kind of sport beyond horseshoes and Carter had too many other diversions on his leisure-time agenda.

It wasn't that the three of them were unfamiliar with the game that steel tycoon Andrew Carnegie once acclaimed as "an indispensable adjunct to high civilization." Far from it. Hoover, for his part, brought a few golfing credentials along with him to the presidency in 1929. He had been a founder and the president of the Congressional Country Club as well as a nonresident member of the Chevy Chase Club. Even so, he never attempted golf at either of those courses in suburban Maryland, although members of his Cabinet frequently did—among them Secretary of State Henry Stimson and Attorney General William D. Mitchell. In fact, Mitchell had one notable distinction as a golfer: He was the first Cabinet member ever to score a hole-in-one.

Fisherman Hoover: He considered fishing a "discipline in the equality of men—for all men are equal before fish." AP/WIDE WORLD PHOTOS

The industrious Hoover permitted himself only two recreational outlets. One was fishing, which he described as a "discipline in the equality of men—for all men are equal before fish." The other outlet was medicine ball. Realizing he needed some form of exercise, Hoover had a medicine ball court laid out on the grounds of the White House. There, various government officials and a few favored journalists joined him each morning at 7:30 for a game strictly limited to half an hour so that no one would be late for work. Hoover and his paunchy playmates were out there—rain or shine, winter or summer—gamely lobbing an eight-pound medicine ball over a 10-foot-high net and using the tennis system to keep score. The participants were facetiously called "Hoover's Medicine Ball Cabinet."

The Truman Alternative

Truman not only didn't play golf, he was actually offended when one newspaper article suggested that he did. It said that, like some wild-hitting antecedent of Gerald Ford, he had struck a bystander on the head with a ball while golfing back home in Independence, Missouri. Truman immediately shot off this denial: "For your information, I have never played golf in my life, never had a golf club in my hands, except to look at it—so I couldn't possibly have fired a ball on the Independence golf course and hit anybody on the head."

Yet like Hoover, he had close ties to a Washington area golf club. As a senator, Truman had grown to know the Burning Tree Club well by walking its course with golfing friends and by sitting in regularly at poker games in the club's lounge. Then, one month

Walker Truman: Brisk walks, at 128 steps a minute, had Secret Service men, not a caddie, scurrying after him. THE KANSAS CITY STAR

after he succeeded Franklin Roosevelt in 1945, Truman received a startling invitation. He was asked to become an honorary member of Burning Tree—the first President to be given that tribute.

Truman accepted and, according to a Burning Tree Club history, he "very graciously entered into the spirit of his honorary membership by attending one of the club parties and made it one of the most memorable evenings in [Burning Tree] history." The President gave "an intimate talk" on the burdens of his office and then climaxed the occasion by hopping over to the piano to play a few solos (including his signature melody, the "Missouri Waltz"). The club saluted him by placing in its caricature gallery a drawing of him that still hangs there.

With his natural combativeness, Truman would have made a fiercely competitive golfer. As Lee Trevino once observed, "He never backed off from anything, and I like that. No way he would ever have been penalized for slow play. He'd just step up and knock the hell out of the ball."

Although Truman might have had the mental toughness needed for competitive golf, he apparently lacked the necessary physical tools. He was never much of an athlete and showed little interest in any game other than horseshoes. Many Presidents had their flings at that pastime, but Truman was the first to have a horseshoe court built at the White House. His keenness so delighted promoters of the game that they gave him some horseshoes plated with bronze and chromium. He realized, though, that horseshoes did little for his physical well-being other than to exercise his left tossing arm. So he developed a three-part fitness regimen that combined walking, gym work and swimming.

Truman strode out each day at 7:00 A.M. for brisk walks (carefully paced at 128 steps per minute) with a Secret Service detail, not a caddie, scurrying to keep up. The two miles that he covered daily were roughly equivalent to walking nine golf holes swiftly and without pause. Before long, however, word about these walks spread, and Truman soon became a kind of Pied Piper of the presidency as reporters, photographers and sightseers trailed behind him. To escape them, he finally arranged for a White House limousine to drive him to various spots on the outskirts of town where he could enjoy his hikes in greater privacy.

When he got back to the White House, Truman would sweat off some poundage in the gym and then do 12 laps (one quarter of a mile) in the indoor pool. He used his own version of a side stroke and held his head out of the water to keep his glasses dry.

Carter's Choices

The third presidential nongolfer, Carter, tried the game briefly as a young man but quickly dropped it, never to resume play again. "Jimmy never took much to golf," a top White House aide said. "He's more of a softball man. He plays tennis a bit, loves fishing and is crazy about auto racing. But golf? Forget it."

The only form of the game that attracted him was Putt-Putt golf, a version of miniature golf he played from time to time. "Mr. Carter is a great friend of Putt-Putt," said an official of the game's

Netman Carter: A gamesman on the tennis court, he psyched out some opponents by calling foot faults on them early in their matches. COURTESY, THE JIMMY CARTER LIBRARY

association shortly before the President's inauguration in 1977. "It will be a wonderful boost to have our game played by the President of the United States."

Putt-Putt golf was still waiting for that boost by the end of Carter's term. He never played a public round while in office. Instead, he gave presidential exposure to the many other sports in which he did participate—including running, tennis, softball, fly-fishing and cross-country skiing.

That exposure, however, was not always the kind that those sports would have invited if they'd had the choice. It was front-page news across the country, for example, when Carter broke his left collarbone while cross-country skiing at Camp David and when he was photographed slumping toward the ground on rubbery legs just before he had to quit a 10-kilometer race in Maryland. The photos of the collapsing Chief Executive dealt an embarrassing blow to his presidential image. To make matters worse, the pictures showed that he was running in black socks.

Nor did he have much better luck with fishing. The story of a "killer" rabbit that once swam out to his boat—he said he had to beat it back with an oar—dogged him for weeks. He later admitted that the incident "gave an image of an incompetent President who couldn't even protect himself from a rabbit." Carter enjoyed more success with softball (he always made sure the Secret Service agents were on his team) and tennis. The micromanagement style he brought to his high office even extended to scheduling the use of the White House tennis court. There, he played a competent game that was occasionally enhanced by some wily gamesmanship.

"He was, by all accounts, very good at psyching out his opponents," said his press secretary, Jody Powell. One of Carter's victims was his national security adviser, Zbigniew Brzezinski, a serious player. "About the third point in Brzezinski's first service game, the President would always call a foot fault on him," Powell reported. "I suspect the President may have called him on a foot fault even if there wasn't a foot fault."

For Carter, Truman and Hoover, golf may indeed have been just "a good walk spoiled." On the other hand, each was elected to only one term as President. So, who knows, it might have been different had they heeded another dictum, this one from British Prime Minister David Lloyd George. "You get to know more of the character of a man in a round of golf," Lloyd George declared, "than you can get to know in six months with only political experience."

CHAPTER 16

HANDICAPPING THE PRESIDENTS

How Do They Rank as Golfers?

C omparing athletes of different eras is an imperfect art at best. Could Muhammad Ali have beaten Jack Dempsey in his prime? Was Bill Tilden's tennis game superior to those of Jimmy Connors and Bjorn Borg? And who was the best golfer: Bobby Jones, Ben Hogan or Jack Nicklaus?

In golf there are mathematical standards by which to judge performance—the players' scores—but, even so, comparing players of different periods poses real difficulties. How would modern golfers, who have the advantage of playing on immaculately groomed courses with today's graphite-shafted clubs and high-powered golf balls, have fared in the midcentury era of steel shafts and fuzzy greens—or, even earlier, in the age of hickory shafts and primitive golf architecture?

The presidential golfers of this century span that huge evolutionary period for the game of golf. William Howard Taft's high-90s scores, for example, look somewhat more respectable when one considers that 1909, when he entered the White House, was the first year anyone ever broke 70 for a single round in the U.S. Open.

However, research comparing players' performance using equipment of the different eras is sparse. One of the few scientific surveys, conducted by *Golf Digest* magazine in 1994, tested modern clubs and modern golf balls against the clubs and balls of some 20 years earlier. Result: Shots with the 1994 equipment flew farther but didn't roll as far; the ball of two decades earlier couldn't be hit as far with the equipment of that day, but shots rolled a greater distance. Net result: Modern equipment helps players, but not nearly so much as might be believed.

Similar conclusions came from a world conference on golf equipment held at St. Andrews, Scotland, in 1994. *The Economist* magazine reported that while the winning score in professional events has been improving by one stroke every 21 years, the pros are not hitting any more fairways or greens in regulation than they did previously. The difference is that professionals are taking fewer putts than they used to. As Frank Thomas, technical director of the U.S. Golf Association, summed it up at the meeting: "Real improvements in golf equipment have happened, but none of these improvements has had a measurable effect on performance." (Thomas hastily added that golf is above all a "mental" game and "what the equipment manufacturers are selling is not a con. It is a temporary aid in the golfer's eternal quest to con himself.")

It is against this background that the authors have made the following ranking of the Presidents as golfers. Reported scores have, of course, been taken into account as have official handicaps, when available. Yet some of these figures, taken on their face value, can be misleading—or even suspect—because of executive privilege and the tendency of playing partners to give extra mulligans and putts considerably outside the leather to the man holding the most important job in the world. Therefore, the authors have also factored in contemporary accounts describing how well—or how badly—each particular President played, his athletic ability and his aptitude for the game. In addition, we also studied old photographs and movies as well as more recent videotapes of the various presidential golf swings.

One may argue about some of these conclusions, but there's no doubt that John F. Kennedy had the best-looking swing of them all.

The Presidential Scorecard

RANK	COMMENTS	STRENGTHS	WEAKNESSES	SCORES
No. 1/ John F. Kennedy	His early start and college golf experience helped make him the best of all presidential golfers—though he tried to keep his affection for the game a state secret.	A graceful, rhythmic swing; accuracy with his shorter irons, particularly his 7-iron; the ability to use games-manship on his opponents.	A bad back often idled him; his impatience made him an indifferent putter.	Rarely played 18 holes but often shot 40 or less for nine. (He probably would have had a handicap in the 7-to-10 range.)
No. 2/ Gerald R. Ford	He learned the game as a youngster, and his athletic ability helped make him a solid performer; a true golf zealot, he virtually retired from the White House to the links.	A big shoulder turn and power that made him exceptionally long off the tee, capable of outdriving professionals; a fiercely competitive nature and dedication to the game.	Erratic shots, particularly when he played before large galleries, which produced much negative publicity; knee injuries from his football days made his swing no thing of beauty.	Was a solid 12 several times during his life and even as he approached the age of 80 had a handicap in the 15-to-17 range.
No. 3/ Dwight D. Eisenhower	A latecomer to the game (he was 37 when he took it up), he became a world-class golf fanatic; used the game as an escape from the heavy duties of the presidency and played an estimated 800 rounds during his two terms.	A serious practice regimen, which saw him spending hours on the White House putting green and hitting long shots inside its fences; an intense competitor; a quality short-iron game; an expert's sense of course management.	An impatient and indifferent putter; a trick knee limited his hip turn and made him a congenital slicer.	Generally a 14-to-18 handi-capper on some tough courses; broke 80 three times during his life.

The Presidential Scorecard (continued)

RANK	COMMENTS	STRENGTHS	WEAKNESSES	SCORES
No. 4/ Franklin D. Roosevelt	He picked up the game while a teenager and once won his club championship; played frequently while serving in the Wilson administration, prior to contracting polio at age 39.	A well-coordinated athlete, with jaunty self-assurance and a powerful swing that produced long drives; his great power made him especially adept at getting out of deep rough.	His great strength was also a weakness; his swing produced distance rather than direction.	Scored in the high 80s fairly consistently.
No. 5/ George Bush	He started playing in his teens, had great golfing genes (his father was a scratch golfer) and delighted in playing very rapidly; his record for 18 holes with a foursome was 1 hour and 42 minutes.	A good all-around athlete (he played varsity baseball and soccer in college); made solid contact with the ball and hit his woods and longer irons with respectable accuracy.	His short game needed work; his putting was even worse—he suffered from a near-fatal case of the yips.	An 11-handicapper when he was younger; the figure soared to twice that during his White House years.
No. 6/ Ronald Reagan	Better known for horseback riding and other outdoor sports, he actually played often and reasonably well during his days as an actor and corporate spokesman; when he entered politics, his golf became more of a social activity.	A powerful, if wristy, swing that he learned as a caddie, which could produce impressive drives and recoveries from the rough; the swing remained serviceable even as he approached 80 years old.	His attitude toward the game was more congenial than competitive; his easy charm and storytelling abilities were more memorable than his shotmaking.	A solid 12 at his peak; once he became President, his game faded.

No. 7/ Richard M. Nixon	Among the least athletic of Presidents, he didn't start playing seriously until he was in his 40s, but his perseverance and determination enabled him to improve rapidly.	A confident putter; his dedicated practice also enabled him to develop a respectable short game.	His awkward swing produced drives that, while accurate, were quite short, usually in the 175- to 200-yard range.	Generally in the low 90s or high 80s, though he once achieved a handicap of 12 prior to his presidential years.
No. 8/ Bill Clinton	Among the more enthusiastic of White House golfers and, unlike some other Democratic Presidents, didn't care who knew about it; ignored many of the game's conventions, with his liberal use of mulligans and his scruffy golf attire when out of public view.	Good balance and a powerful swing, capable of cranking out long drives; an amiable companion on the links, he freely offered compliments to opponents.	A flying elbow and unorthodox posture at the top of his backswing made his game fairly inconsistent; he also offended purists with his slow play, often taking five hours or more for a round.	Sometimes credited with a handicap in the low teens; it was probably closer to 20. Scored in the 80s or low 90s, depending on how many mulligans he took.
No. 9/ William Howard Taft	Despite his great girth and primitive, turn-of-the-century equipment, he played a respectable game—and his widely publicized affection for golf helped trigger its first boom in America.	A good putter, with great powers of concentration; an abiding passion for the game.	In addition to his colossal size, he gripped the club as if it were a baseball bat; had a short, choppy swing.	Generally in the middle to high 90s.
No. 10/ Warren G. Harding	A committed golfer who played in fair weather and foul, he was one of those rare players who didn't let the game's vagaries upset him; he enjoyed the camaraderie as much as the game itself.	A smooth, effective putting stroke; short pitches to the green.	A two-thirds swing, due to an abbreviated takeaway and an equally short follow-through; that, plus a tendency to rush his swing, produced mediocre results.	Struggled to break 100, though he did so on occasion; a career best of 92.

The Presidential Scorecard (continued)

RANK	COMMENTS	STRENGTHS	WEAKNESSES	SCORES
No. 11/ Woodrow Wilson	He golfed often (up to six times a week in summer during his Washington years) but not well; never much of an athlete, he embraced the game when he was in his 40s, on his doctor's orders.	Not many, even though his short game and putting were fairly respectable; he was courteous on the course, declining to play through other foursomes.	A fidgety player, with a baseball grip and a minimal follow-through; a wicked slice.	Rarely, if ever, broke 100; generally shot around 115.
No. 12/ Lyndon B. Johnson	A devotee of the hit-'til-you're-happy school of golf, he hit extra shots as if they were part of the game; like John Kennedy, he tried to hide the fact that he played golf.	An amiable golfing companion, who often used the links for political ends; could uncork long (but often wild) drives.	Relatively little athletic ability and a lack of aptitude for the game; he moved his hands too early from the top of his swing and often took huge divots.	He never broke 100 with his initial ball.
No. 13/ Calvin Coolidge	He recognized golf's benefits as a means of relaxation but remained the least competent of all presidential golfers; his attire—often street clothes—was as incongruous as his game.	The only President who golfed left-handed, he had none to speak of.	Was extremely short off the tee and pecked away at his fairway shots; displayed an almost total lack of interest in the game or any sport.	Astronomical; once took 11 strokes to reach a par 3.

Bibliography

General References

BOOKS

Burning Tree Club, A History 1922–1962. Bethesda, Md.: privately printed, 1962.

Burning Tree Club, The Fifth Decade 1963–1972. Bethesda, Md.: privately printed, 1972.

Cornish, Geoffrey S., and Ronald E. Whitten. *The Golf Course*. New York: The Rutledge Press, 1981.

Dolan, Anne Reilly. *Congressional Country Club, 1924–1984*. Washington, D.C.: privately printed, 1984.

DeGregorio, William A. *The Complete Book of U.S. Presidents.* New York and Avenel, N.J.: Wings Books, 1991.

Hope, Bob, with Dwayne Netland. *Confessions of a Hooker. My Lifelong Affair with Golf*. Garden City, N.Y.: Doubleday, 1985.

Lindrop, Edmund, and Joseph Jares. *White House Sportsmen*. Boston: Houghton Mifflin, 1964.

Lynham, John M. *The Chevy Chase Club, A History. 1885–1957*. Chevy Chase, Md.: privately printed, 1958.

Martin, Harry B. *Fifty Years of American Golf*. New York: Dodd Mead, 1936.

Udall, Morris K. *Too Funny To Be President*. New York: Henry Holt, 1988.

U.S. Golf Association. *Golf: The Greatest Game*. New York: HarperCollins, 1994.

Wind, Herbert Warren. *The Story of American Golf*. New York: Farrar, Straus, 1948.

OTHER SOURCES THAT WERE CONSULTED FOR MANY CHAPTERS

The Associated Press.

Newspapers: *The New York Times, USA Today, The Washington Post*.

Magazines: *The American Golfer, Golf, Golf Digest, Golf Journal, Sports Illustrated, Time, U.S. News & World Report*.

Television: ESPN, *All the Presidents' Games,* October 27, 1992.

Chapter 1: Introduction

Allen, Sir Peter. *The Sunley Book of Royal Golf*. London: Stanley Paul, 1989.

Browning, Robert. *A History of Golf*. London: J. M. Dent and Sons, 1955.

Catton, Bruce. *U.S. Grant: The American Military Tradition*. Boston: Little, Brown and Company, 1954.

Cromie, Robert. *Par for the Course*. New York: Macmillan, 1964.

Johnston, Alastair J. and James F. *The Chronicles of Golf: 1457 to 1857*. Cleveland, Ohio: privately published, 1993.

Schwartz, Gary H. *The Art of Golf 1754–1940*. Tiburon, Calif.: Wood River, 1990.

Snead, Sam, with George Mendoza. *Slammin' Sam*. New York: Donald I. Fine, 1986.

Travers, Jerome D., and James R. Crowell. *The Fifth Estate. Thirty Years of Golf*. New York: Alfred A. Knopf, 1926.

Trevino, Lee, and Sam Blair. *The Snake in the Sandtrap*. New York: Holt, Rinehart and Winston, 1985.

Wodehouse, P. G. *The Heart of a Goof*. London: Penguin Books, 1982.

Woodward, W. E. *Meet General Grant*. New York: Horace Liveright, 1928.

Additional sources: *The Boston Evening Record, Collier's, Golfiana, Hello!, Life, Newsweek, The Saturday Evening Post.*

Chapter 2: William Howard Taft

Anderson, Judith Icke. *William Howard Taft, An Intimate History*. New York: W. W. Norton, 1981.

Butt, Archibald. *Taft and Roosevelt, The Intimate Letters of Archie Butt*. Garden City, N.Y.: Doubleday, Doran and Company, 1930.

Cotton, Edward H. *William Howard Taft—A Character Study*. Boston: The Beacon Press, 1932.

Lauder, Sir Harry. *Roamin' in the Gloamin'*. London: Hutchinson, 1928.

Pringle, Henry F. *The Life and Times of William Howard Taft. Volume 2*. New York: Farrar and Rinehart, 1939.

Travers, Jerome D., and James R. Crowell. *The Fifth Estate. Thirty Years of Golf*. New York: Alfred A. Knopf, 1926.

Additional sources: *The Century, Collier's, Everybody's Magazine, Golf Course Management, Golf Illustrated, Hampton's, Harper's Weekly, The Independent, The Met Golfer, The Ohio State Journal, The Saturday Evening Post, The Savannah Press, Scribner's.*

Chapter 3: Woodrow Wilson

Alsop, EM Bowles, editor. *The Greatness of Woodrow Wilson*. New York: Rinehart, 1956.

Baker, Ray Stannard. *Woodrow Wilson, Life and Letters. Vols. 2, 4, 5 and 8*. Garden City, N.Y.: Doubleday, Page, 1927–1939.

Bell, H.C.F. *Woodrow Wilson and the People*. Garden City, N.Y.: Doubleday, Doran, 1945.

Clements, Kendrick A. *Woodrow Wilson, World Statesman*. Boston: Twayne, 1987.

Daniels, Josephus. *The Wilson Era, Years of War and After. 1917–1923*. Chapel Hill: University of North Carolina Press, 1946.

Evans, Chick. *The Chick Evans Golf Book*. Chicago: Published for Thomas E. Wilson by Reilly and Lee, 1921.

Graffis, Herb. *The PGA*. New York: Thomas Y. Crowell, 1975.

Grayson, Rear Admiral Gary T. *Woodrow Wilson: An Intimate Memoir*. New York: Holt, Rinehart and Winston, 1960.

Hatch, Alden. *Edith Bolling Wilson: First Lady Extraordinary*. New York: Dodd, Mead, 1961.

Hoover, Irwin Hood ("Ike"). *Forty-two Years in the White House*. Boston: Houghton Mifflin, 1934.

Lewis, McMillan. *Woodrow Wilson of Princeton*. Narberth, Pa.: Livingston, 1952.

McAdoo, Eleanor Wilson, with Margaret Y. Gaffey. *The Woodrow Wilsons*. New York: Macmillan, 1937.

Mulder, John M. *Woodrow Wilson: The Years of Preparation*. Princeton, N.J.: Princeton University Press, 1978.

Ross, Ishbel. *Power with Grace: The Life Story of Mrs. Woodrow Wilson*. New York: G. P. Putnam's Sons, 1975.

Shachtman, Tom. *Edith and Woodrow: A Presidential Romance*. New York: G. P. Putnam's Sons, 1981.

Smith, Gene. *When the Cheering Stopped: The Last Years of Woodrow Wilson*. New York: William Morrow, 1964.

Starling, Colonel Edmund W. *Starling of the White House*. New York: Simon and Schuster, 1946.

Tumulty, Joseph P. *Woodrow Wilson As I Knew Him*. New York: Doubleday, Page, 1921.

Walworth, Arthur. *Woodrow Wilson I: American Prophet*. New York: Longmans, Green, 1958.

White, William Allen. *Woodrow Wilson: The Man, His Times and His Task*. Boston: Houghton Mifflin, 1924.

Winkler, John K. *Woodrow Wilson: The Man Who Lives On*. New York: The Vanguard Press, 1933.

Wilson, Edith Bolling. *My Memoir*. Indianapolis, Ind.: Bobbs-Merrill, 1938.

Woodmont Country Club: A History. 1913–1988. Rockville, Md.: privately printed, 1988.

Additional sources: *The Literary Digest, The Saturday Evening Post.*

Chapter 4: Warren G. Harding

Adams, Samuel Hopkins. *Incredible Era: The Life and Times of Warren Gamaliel Harding.* Boston: Houghton Mifflin, 1939.

Daughtery, Harry. *The Inside Story of the Harding Tragedy.* New York: Churchill, 1932.

Downes, R. C. *The Rise of Warren Gamaliel Harding.* Columbus: Ohio State University Press, 1970.

Hoover, Irwin Hood ("Ike"). *Forty-two Years in the White House.* Boston: Houghton Mifflin, 1934.

Johnson, Willis Fletcher. *The Life of Warren G. Harding.* Chicago: John C. Winston, 1923.

Lauder, Sir Harry. *Roamin' in the Gloamin'.* London: Hutchinson, 1928.

Mee, C. L., Jr. *The Ohio Gang.* New York: M. Evans, 1981.

Mitchell, Joe. *The Life and Times of Warren G. Harding.* Boston: Chapple, 1924.

Murray, Robert K. *The Harding Era.* Minneapolis: University of Minnesota Press, 1969.

Russell, Francis. *The Shadow of Blooming Grove.* New York: McGraw-Hill, 1968.

Smith, Gene. *When the Cheering Stopped: The Last Years of Woodrow Wilson.* New York: William Morrow, 1964.

Starling, Colonel Edmund W. *Starling of the White House.* New York: Simon and Schuster, 1946.

Traini, E. P., and D. L. Wilson. *The Presidency of Warren G. Harding.* Regents Press of Kansas, 1977.

Additional sources: *Golf Course Management, Golf Illustrated, Golf Journal, The Literary Digest, The Met Golfer, The Saturday Evening Post.*

Chapter 5: Calvin Coolidge

Harbaugh, William H. *Lawyer's Lawyer, The Life of John W. Davis.* New York: Oxford University Press, 1973.

Hennessy, M. E. *Calvin Coolidge.* New York: G. P. Putnam's Sons, 1924.

Hoover, Irwin Hood ("Ike"). *Forty-two Years in the White House.* Boston: Houghton Mifflin, 1934.

Mosedale, John. *The Greatest of Them All: the '27 Yankees.* New York: Dial, 1974.

Ross, Ishbel. *Grace Coolidge and Her Era.* New York: Dodd, Mead, 1962.

Russell, Francis. *The Shadow of Blooming Grove.* New York: McGraw-Hill, 1968.

Smith, Richard Norton. *An Uncommon Man: The Triumph of Herbert Hoover.* New York: Simon and Schuster, 1964.

Starling, Colonel Edmund W. *Starling of the White House.* New York: Simon and Schuster, 1946.

Chapter 6: Franklin D. Roosevelt

Burns, James MacGregor. *Roosevelt: The Lion and the Fox.* New York: Harcourt, Brace, Jovanovich, 1956.

Busch, Noel F. *What Manner of Man?* New York: Harper, 1944.

Hatch, Alden. *Franklin D. Roosevelt: An Informal Biography.* New York: Henry Holt, 1947.

Lindley, Ernest K. *Franklin D. Roosevelt: A Career in Progressive Democracy.* Indianapolis, Ind.: Bobbs-Merrill, 1931.

Maine, Basil. *Franklin Roosevelt: His Life and Achievements.* London: John Murray, 1938.

McIntire, Vice Admiral Ross T. *White House Physician.* New York: G. P. Putnam's Sons, 1946.

Ross, Leland M., and Allen W. Grobin. *This Democratic Roosevelt: The Life Story of "F.D."* New York: E. P. Dutton, 1932.

Roosevelt, Eleanor. *This Is My Story.* New York: Harper, 1937.

Roosevelt, Elliott, editor. *F.D.R. His Personal Letters*. New York: Duell, Sloan and Pearce, 1947.

Roosevelt, James, and Sidney Shalett. *Affectionately, F.D.R.: A Son's Story of a Lonely Man*. New York: Harcourt, Brace, 1959.

Roosevelt, Mrs. James. *My Boy, Franklin*. New York: Ray Long and Richard R. Smith, 1933.

Smith, Gene. *When the Cheering Stopped: The Last Years of Woodrow Wilson*. New York: William Morrow, 1964.

Tugwell, Rexford G. *The Democratic Roosevelt*. Garden City, N.Y.: Doubleday, 1957.

Ward, Geoffrey C. *Before the Trumpet: Young Franklin Roosevelt 1882–1905*. New York: Harper and Row, 1985.

————. *A First-Class Temperament: The Emergence of Franklin Roosevelt*. New York: Harper and Row, 1989.

Additional sources: *Maine Golf, The Orlando Sentinel*.

Chapter 7: Dwight D. Eisenhower

Brendon, Piers. *Ike: His Life and Times*. London: Secker and Warburg, 1987.

Butler, Paul F. *Presidential Anecdotes*. New York: Oxford University Press, 1981.

Eisenhower, Dwight D. *At Ease: Stories I Tell to Friends*. Garden City, N.Y.: Doubleday, 1967.

Eisenhower, John. *Strictly Personal*. Garden City, N.Y.: Doubleday, 1974.

Larson, Arthur. *The President Nobody Knew: Eisenhower as a Person*. New York: Charles Scribner's Sons, 1968.

Lyon, Peter. *Eisenhower: Portrait of a Hero*. Boston: Little, Brown and Company, 1974.

McCormack, Mark H. *Arnie: The Evolution of a Legend*. New York: Simon and Schuster, 1967.

Menzies, Gordon, editor. *The World of Golf*. London: British Broadcasting Corporation, 1982.

Neal, Steve. *The Eisenhowers: Reluctant Dynasty*. Garden City, N.Y.: Doubleday, 1978.

Palmer, Norman, and William V. Levy. *Five Star Golf.* New York: Duell, Sloan and Pierce, 1964.

Schumacher, Alan T. *The Newport Country Club: Its Curious History.* Newport, R.I.: privately printed, 1986.

Snead, Sam, with George Mendoza. *Slammin' Sam.* New York: Donald I. Fine, 1986.

Tolhurst, Desmond. *Golf at Merion.* Ardmore, Pa: privately printed, 1989.

West, J. B. *Upstairs at the White House: My Life with First Ladies.* New York: Warner, 1973.

Additional sources: *The Baltimore Sun, Chicago Tribune, Collier's, The Danbury News-Times, Golf Course Management, Golf World, Look, The Met Golfer, Newsweek, The New York Herald-Tribune, Parade, The Saturday Evening Post, The Sporting News.*

Chapter 8: John F. Kennedy

Blair, Joan, and Clay Blair Jr. *The Search for JFK.* New York: Berkley, 1976.

Bradlee, Benjamin C. *Conversations with Kennedy.* New York: W. W. Norton, 1975.

Damore, Leo. *The Cape Cod Years of John Fitzgerald Kennedy.* Englewood Cliffs, N.J.: Prentice-Hall, 1967.

Fay, Paul B., Jr. *The Pleasure of His Company.* New York: Harper and Row, 1966.

Lasky, Victor. *JFK: The Man and the Myth.* New York: Macmillan, 1963.

Manchester, William. *Portrait of a President: John F. Kennedy in Profile.* Boston: Little, Brown and Company, 1967.

O'Donnell, Kenneth P., and David Powers, with Joe McCarthy. *"Johnny, We Hardly Knew Ye."* Boston: Little, Brown and Company, 1970.

Reeves, Richard. *President Kennedy: Profile of Power.* New York: Simon and Schuster, 1993.

Reeves, Thomas C. *A Question of Character: A Life of John F. Kennedy*. Rocklin, Calif.: Prima, 1992.

Salinger, Pierre. *With Kennedy*. Garden City, N.Y.: Doubleday, 1966.

Additional sources: *The Economist, Golf Course Management*.

Chapter 9: Lyndon B. Johnson

Califano, Joseph A., Jr. *The Triumph and Tragedy of Lyndon Johnson: The White House Years*. New York: Simon and Schuster, 1991.

Dugger, Ronnie. *The Politician: The Life and Times of Lyndon Johnson*. New York: W. W. Norton, 1982.

McCormack, Mark H. *Arnie: The Evolution of a Legend*. New York: Simon and Schuster, 1967.

Provence, Harry. *Lyndon B. Johnson: A Biography*. New York: Fleet, 1964.

Reedy, George. *Lyndon Johnson: A Memoir*. New York: Andrews and McMeel, 1982.

Worley, Eugene. *Golf Game with Lyndon Johnson*. From The Lyndon Baines Johnson Library's Oral History Collection, Austin, Tex., 1968.

Additional sources: *Los Angeles Times, The Sporting News*.

Chapter 10: Richard M. Nixon

Ambrose, Stephen E. *Nixon: The Education of a Politician, 1913–1962*. New York: Simon and Schuster, 1987.

Blackburn, Norman. *Lakeside Golf Club of Hollywood: 50th Anniversary Book*. Burbank, Calif.: Cal-Ad, 1974.

Brodie, Fawn M. *Richard Nixon: The Shaping of his Character*. New York: W. W. Norton, 1981.

Buchanan, Patrick J. *Right from the Beginning*. Boston: Little, Brown and Company, 1988.

Frady, Marshall. *Billy Graham: A Parable of American Righteousness*. Boston: Little, Brown and Company, 1979.

Hughes, Arthur J. *Richard M. Nixon*. New York: Dodd, Mead, 1972.

Mahon, James J. *Baltusrol, 90 Years in the Mainstream of American Golf*. Plainfield, N.J.: privately printed, 1985.

Miller, Richard. *The Town and Country World of Golf*. Dallas, Tex.: Taylor, 1992.

Nixon, Richard M. *In the Arena: A Memoir of Victory, Defeat and Renewal*. New York: Simon and Schuster, 1990.

Penna, Toney, with Oscar Fraley. *My Wonderful World of Golf*. New York: Centaur House, 1965.

Pollock, John. *Billy Graham*. New York: Harper and Row, 1979.

Snead, Sam, with George Mendoza. *Slammin' Sam*. New York: Donald I. Fine, 1986.

Additional sources: *The Journal of Sports History, The National Sports Daily, Newsweek, Vanity Fair.*

Chapter 11: Gerald R. Ford

Boller, Paul F. *Presidential Anecdotes*. New York: Oxford University Press, 1981.

Cannon, James. *Time and Chance: Gerald Ford's Appointment with History*. New York: HarperCollins, 1994.

Ford, Betty, with Chris Chase. *The Times of My Life*. New York: Harper and Row, 1978.

Trevino, Lee, and Sam Blair. *The Snake in the Sandtrap*. New York: Holt, Rinehart and Winston, 1985.

Snead, Sam, with George Mendoza. *Slammin' Sam*. New York: Donald I. Fine, 1986.

Vestal, Bud. *Jerry Ford Up Close: An Investigative Biography*. New York: Coward, McCann and Geoghegan, 1974.

Additional source: *The Saturday Evening Post.*

Chapter 12: Ronald Reagan

Adler, Bill. *Ronnie and Nancy: A Very Special Love Story.* New York: Crown, 1985.

Bauer, Stephen M., with Frances Spatz Leighton. *At Ease in the White House: The Uninhibited Memoirs of a Presidential Social Aide.* New York: Carol, 1991.

Boller, Paul F. *Presidential Anecdotes.* New York: Oxford University Press, 1981.

Cannon, Lou. *President Reagan: The Role of a Lifetime.* New York: Simon and Schuster, 1991.

Edwards, Anne. *Early Reagan: The Rise to Power.* New York: William Morrow, 1987.

Reagan, Ronald, with Richard G. Hubler. *Ronald Reagan's Own Story: Where's the Rest of Me?* New York: Karz-Segil, 1981.

Shultz, George P. *Turmoil and Triumph: My Years as Secretary of State.* New York: Charles Scribner's Sons, 1993.

Van Der Linden, Frank. *The Real Reagan.* New York: William Morrow, 1981.

Additional sources: *Los Angeles Times, Newsweek, Parade.*

Chapter 13: George Bush

Bauer, Stephen M., with Frances Spatz Leighton. *At Ease in the White House: The Uninhibited Memoirs of a Presidential Social Aide.* New York: Carol, 1991.

Additional sources: *The Baltimore Sun, The Dallas Morning News, The Danbury News-Times, The Economist, Golf Illustrated, Golf Life, Golf Market Today, Golf World, Links, Maine Golf, Manhattan Inc., The Myrtle Beach Sun-News, New York Post, Newsweek, New York, The New Yorker, Parade, People, The Sporting News, Tennis.*

Chapter 14: Bill Clinton

Levin, Robert E. *Bill Clinton: The Inside Story.* New York: S.P.I. Books, 1992.

Additional sources: *The Boston Herald, The Detroit News, Esquire, Golf World, The Myrtle Beach Sun-News, The New Yorker, Parade, People, PGA Magazine, San Francisco Chronicle, USA Weekend.*

Chapter 15: Herbert Hoover, Harry Truman, Jimmy Carter

Bauer, Stephen M., with Frances Spatz Leighton. *At Ease in the White House: The Uninhibited Memoirs of a Presidential Social Aide.* New York: Carol, 1991.

Hoover, Herbert. *The Memoirs of.* New York: Macmillan, 1953.

Hoover, Irwin Hood ("Ike"). *Forty-two Years in the White House.* Boston: Houghton Mifflin, 1934.

Lyons, Eugene. *Herbert Hoover: A Biography.* Garden City, N.Y.: Doubleday, 1964.

Smith, Richard Norton. *An Uncommon Man: The Triumph of Herbert Hoover.* New York: Simon and Schuster, 1964.

Starling, Colonel Edmund W. *Starling of the White House.* New York: Simon and Schuster, 1946.

Steinberg, Alfred. *The Man from Missouri: The Life and Times of Harry Truman.* New York: G. P. Putnam's Sons, 1962.

Truman, Margaret. *Bess W. Truman.* New York: Macmillan, 1986.

West, J. B. *Upstairs at the White House: My Life with First Ladies.* New York: Warner, 1973.

Additional sources: *The Danbury News-Times, The Denver Post, The Literary Digest.*

Acknowledgments

The authors are deeply grateful to several former Presidents and a former First Lady for their cooperation. Richard M. Nixon, Gerald R. Ford, Ronald Reagan, George Bush and Lady Bird Johnson were all generous with their time and forthcoming with their thoughts in answering our questions. Their responses gave us a special insight into why golf is the sport of Presidents.

We also received invaluable assistance in our research from the various presidential libraries. Those who were particularly helpful included Maryanne Gerbauckas at the William Howard Taft National Historic Site in Cincinnati, Ohio; Frank Aucella at the Woodrow Wilson House in Washington, D.C.; John Ferris and Susan Elter at the Franklin D. Roosevelt Library in Hyde Park, New York; Benedict K. Zobrist and Pauline Testerman at the Harry Truman Library in Independence, Missouri; Dennis H.J. Medina and Marion Kamm at the Dwight D. Eisenhower Library in Abilene, Kansas; Betty Tilson at the Lyndon B. Johnson Library in Austin, Texas; Susan Naulty at the Richard Nixon Library in Yorba Linda, California; Scott P. Houting at the Gerald R. Ford Museum in Grand Rapids, Michigan, and Kenneth G. Hafeli at the Gerald R. Ford Library in Ann Arbor, Michigan; Martin Elzy and David Stanhope at the Jimmy Carter Library in Atlanta, Georgia; and Ron Soubers, Kelly D. Barton and Cathy Sewell at the Ronald Reagan Library in Simi Valley, California.

Similar support was provided by the staffs at the incomparable New York City Public Library, the National Archives in Washington,

D.C., the South Carolina State Library in Columbia, the Ohio Historical Society in Columbus, the University Club Library in New York City, the U.S. Golf Association in Far Hills, New Jersey, as well as the following facilities in Connecticut: The Yale University libraries in New Haven, the *Golf Digest* library in Trumbull and the public libraries in Stamford, Westport and Ridgefield.

Beyond that, we are indebted to a number of individuals whose guidance, encouragement and assistance—which took many forms—were indispensable in making this book possible. We'd especially like to thank:

- Gilbert E. Kaplan for helping us shape the idea and for his wisdom and support;
- Former U.S. Senator J. Glenn Beall for his introductions and for guiding us through the bureaucratic labyrinths of Washington, D.C.;
- Herbert Warren Wind, the golf writer and historian, for his suggestions and insights into the field of golf literature;
- Tina Aridas of *Institutional Investor* for acting as our initial copy editor and for all of her intelligent comments that went far beyond grammar;
- Stephanie Cross and Gary Walters of the White House for handling our inquiries with such professionalism.

We benefited, too, from the introductions furnished by Daniel Burke of Capital Cities/ABC, William Safire of *The New York Times*, journalist-biographer Cary Reich and artist Roy Doty. Our research was also advanced by leads produced by many other people, most notably Louis Auer, Ronald T. Gault, Robert E. Connor, Joe Louis Barrow and Biddle Worthington.

A number of journalists helped us out, among them Jerry Tarde, Peter Andrews, Bob Carney, Lois Haines and Hope Johnson of *Golf Digest,* George Peper of *Golf* magazine and Bob Labbance of *Vermont Golf*. Ted Slate of *Newsweek* allowed us, as former staffers, to peruse the magazine's morgue files. Two members of the Golf Collectors' Society, Joseph S.F. Murdoch and Richard E. Donovan, were particularly encouraging. And Karen J. Bednarski and Andrew Mutch of the U.S. Golf Association were most kind with their time and assistance.

Since photography plays such an important role in this book, special thanks are also due Chel Dong and Helen Cannavale of *Institutional Investor*'s art department, Marcia Lien of AP/Wide World Photos and Debbie Goodsite of UPI/Bettmann.

We are also grateful to Ngaere Macray, Peter Schwed and Gail Eltringham for sharing their knowledge of the publishing field, to Joe Freedman of Sarabande Press for putting us on the right publishing track, to James Blackwell and Dick Squires for giving us wise counsel, to Carol Stewart for pitching in with such competence and to Clem Morgello for the important part he played in both the authors' literary careers.

Further thanks go to Neil Reshen, who acted as our agent; to Jeanine Bucek, our editor at Macmillan Books, who handled our prose with grace and understanding; and to the design and production people at Macmillan, especially Carol McKenna, who helped put it all together.

And a special role was played by Jennifer Campbell, whose belief in this book and whose warm, steadfast support were more instrumental in making it possible than she realized.

March 1996

Shepherd Campbell
Peter Landau

Index

Page numbers in *italics* refer to photographs or illustrations.

Weeks, John W., 60

Weill, Sanford, 177

Weintraub, Jerry, 196

Westland, Rep. Jack, 125

Whitehead, Allen
"Napoleon," 110

Whyte, William, 178

Wilson, Edith Bolling,
40, 42, 44, 46–49,
49, 50

Wilson, Ellen, 40

Wilson, Grady, 161

Wilson, Prime Minister
Harold, 143

Wilson, Woodrow, 30,
59, 66, 81, 86, 87

ability, 37, 38, 40, 42

attitude, 35, 37–39, 40

charity golf balls, 47

Chevy Chase Club con-
troversy, 43

on course, 41, 42, 46

crises when golfing,
35–37

criticism, 41

defense of play, 41

definition of golf, 38

equipment, 37

first played, 39, 40

frequency of play, 37

health, 39, 40, 47

humor, 40–42, 46

as partner, 39, 40–42

Princeton and, 35, 39

putting, 38, *41*

ranking among Presi-
dents, 248

reclusive golfer, 41

Roosevelt, Franklin D.
and, 86, 87

scores, 37, 38, 248

short game, 37

strengths, 37, 38, 248

swing, 37

temperament, 41, 42

weaknesses, 37, 248

war-time golf,
44, 46

why played, 40

Windsor, Duke of, 6, 7,
39

Woodmont C.C., 43

World Golf Hall of
Fame, 171, 176

Worley, Rep. Eugene,
144, 145

Wyman, Jane, 190

Y

Yeltsin, Boris, 9

York, Duchess of, 8

York, Duke of, 7